Meeting special needs
in primary settings

Special needs handbook

IDENTIFYING NEEDS • BUILDING CONFIDENCE • SUPPORTING COLLEAGUES • WORKING WITH FAMILIES

DR HANNAH MORTIMER

Author
Dr Hannah Mortimer

Editor
Victoria Lee

Assistant Editor
Aileen Lalor

Series Designers
Sarah Rock/Anna Oliwa

Designers
Andrea Lewis/Erik Ivens

Illustrations
Debbie Clark

Cover artwork
Richard Johnson

Acknowledgements
Extracts from the Education Act 1944, as amended by the Children Act 1989 © Crown Copyright
Thanks to Johan Welsh, Aysgarth School, for allowing use of her individual IEP format.

Every effort has been made to trace copyright holders and the publishers apologise for any inadvertent omissions.

Text © 2004, Hannah Mortimer
© 2004, Scholastic Ltd

Designed using Adobe InDesign
Published by Scholastic Ltd, Villiers House,
Clarendon Avenue, Leamington Spa, Warwickshire CV32 5PR

Visit our website at www.scholastic.co.uk

Printed by Bell & Bain Ltd, Glasgow

1 2 3 4 5 6 7 8 9 0   4 5 6 7 8 9 0 1 2 3

British Library Cataloguing-in-Publication Data A catalogue record for this book is available from the British Library.

ISBN 0 439 971616

Special Needs Handbook

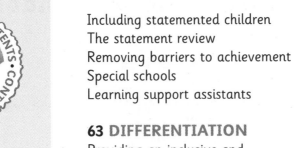

INTRODUCTION

All teaching staff are responsible for meeting the needs of the children they work with. This book is the handbook of a series which will give you practical ideas for welcoming children with special educational needs to your school.

Aims of the series

The DfES has published a revised Code of Practice for the identification and assessment of special educational needs. It provides you with new guidance on how to include children who have disabilities. In addition, the National Numeracy and National Literacy Strategies emphasise the key role that teachers play in making sure that the curriculum is accessible to all pupils. The Government's strategy for SEN includes a whole framework of initiatives to remove barriers to pupils' achievement and we are now beginning to see 'joined up' policies that

can make real differences to children. This series gives suggestions to class teachers and others working in schools on how to meet and monitor special educational needs (SEN) under the new guidelines. It provides accessible information and advice for class teachers and subject teachers at Key Stage 1 and Key Stage 2. The activity books will also provide practical examples of how teachers can use this information to plan inclusive teaching across all areas of the National Curriculum. Finally, there will be a strong emphasis throughout on the importance of maintaining children's self-esteem and confidence despite any learning difficulty they might have.

There is related legislation and guidance in Wales, Scotland and Northern Ireland though the detail and terminology is rather different. For example, the 'statement' of SEN in England and Wales is called a 'Record' in Scotland. Nevertheless, the general approaches and information covered in this book will be relevant throughout the UK.

About the series

Within this *Special Needs in the Primary Years* series, there are three books on helping children with most kinds of special need:
● *Special Needs Handbook*, which supplies general information for SENCOs or class teachers to help meet all the special educational needs in the school or class
● *The Essential A–Z Guide to Special Needs*, which provides basic information for class teachers and support assistants
● *Activities for Including Children with Behavioural Difficulties*, which suggests a range of practical activities for including these children in the primary curriculum.

Who this book is for

This book is principally for teachers and support assistants who work on a daily basis with the children. It will provide a first point of reference for understanding SEN and will be helpful to have to hand in a busy classroom. Each school is required to appoint a special educational needs co-ordinator (or 'SENCO') who will act as the contact point for all SEN matters, and this book will also be helpful for SENCOs, head teachers and governors to use with the staff they work with.

The SENCO's role is to support their colleagues in meeting SEN in their schools, though it is the responsibility of *each staff member* to support children in their classes who have SEN. This *Special Needs Handbook* will help SENCOs provide colleagues with the general information they need about terms, issues and guidelines, all in one place for easy reference. SENCOs are busy people and cannot always be present when a member of staff needs quick and basic information. This book can serve as a helpful starting point for staff who can then contact the SENCO for further information and detail as needed, leaning on the other books in this series. Many SENCOs are also taking on a new role in ensuring equal opportunities within their schools and this book contains basic information that will support this additional role. Finally, the book will also be a useful reference for parents, carers, and trainees.

How to use the book

You are not expected to be an expert on SEN. You already have an expertise in individual children, how they learn, their strengths and their weaknesses. This book provides you with the very basics, so that you can be familiar enough with the issues and approaches to be able to make the right assessments and plan appropriate interventions. Read through the book to provide yourself with a basic level of knowledge and then dip into sections for quick reference. You should also have available and be familiar with the SEN *Code of Practice* and the *SEN Toolkit* (DfES). The SENCO will have copies of these.

In the first chapter, you will think about the meaning of 'inclusion' and how you can plan inclusively for the needs of all your pupils. Chapter 2 provides information on how to decide whether or not a child has special educational needs and how to assess these. Once you have identified SEN in a pupil, Chapter 3 helps you to plan additional and different interventions, and Chapter 4 describes what might happen next if the child still does not make acceptable progress.

Some of the practicalities of providing a differentiated and inclusive curriculum are covered in Chapter 5 and you will find that the activity books in this series complement those approaches. In Chapter 6 there are ideas for making sure the children themselves feel involved in their SEN monitoring. The rationale for working with parents is covered in Chapter 7, and there are pointers for working with other agencies and professionals in the final chapter.

Throughout the book you will find photocopiable pages, which include assessment sheets, record-keeping formats, child questionnaires for reviews, parent letters, explanation leaflets for parents, carers and pupils, and a jargon buster. There is a list of resources, organisations and agencies at the end of the book.

Legal requirements

All schools are required to follow the SEN Code of Practice. There are also coloured sections of text that you are obliged to fulfil by law. The Code is a guide for school governors, schools and local education authorities (LEAs) about the help they can give to children with special educational needs. It recommends that schools identify children's needs and take action to meet those needs as early as possible, working with parents and carers. The aim is to enable all pupils with SEN to reach their full potential, to be included fully in their school communities and to make a successful transition to adulthood.

Taking action

It is recognised that good practice can take many forms, and schools are encouraged to adopt a flexible and a graduated response to the SEN of individual children. This approach recognises that there is a continuum of SEN and, where necessary, brings increasing specialist expertise on board if the child is experiencing continuing difficulties. Once a child's SEN have been identified, the providers should intervene through 'School Action'. This intervention is co-ordinated by the SENCO. However, each teacher in the school shares the responsibility of intervening to support the child.

When reviewing the child's progress and the help they are receiving, the teacher might decide to seek alternative approaches to learning through the help of the outside support services. These interventions are known as 'School Action Plus'. School Action Plus is characterised by the involvement of specialists from outside the school, usually through the local LEA support service. For a very few children, the help provided by School Action Plus will still not be sufficient to ensure satisfactory progress. The school staff, external professional and parents may then decide to ask the LEA to consider carrying out a statutory assessment of the child's SEN, possibly leading to a 'statement'. About one in six children might be expected to have SEN at some stage in their school career, and some may require special action to be taken at one point and then no longer need it at another. Only about two in a hundred pupils go on to receive a statement of SEN and this figure is decreasing as more support becomes delegated to schools. Each maintained school now has a budget for meeting the SEN of the pupils and this should be earmarked for those children. However, *special support* need not mean *individual help* and that budget should be used in a flexible way to make sure a child with SEN is included in the curriculum as far as possible.

Meeting SEN inclusively

'Inclusion' is the practice of including all children together in a school. All children participate fully in all the regular routines and activities of the classroom and school day, though these might need to be modified to meet individual children's goals and teaching targets. There are certain common features that promote inclusion.

● There is usually careful joint planning. For example, if there is special support for a child, how will it be used? Will the child still have access to the full range of adults, children and learning activities?

● Staff use educational labels rather than categories or medical labels, such as 'a child who has epilepsy', rather than 'an epileptic' or 'a child who has SEN' rather than 'an SEN child'.

● School staff provide good role models because of their positive expectations and the way they respect and value the children.

● Special attention is given to improving children's access and communication skills.

● Teaching strategies are developed which enable *all* children to participate and to learn.

● Approaches are planned which draw on pupils' earlier experiences, set high expectations, and encourage mutual peer support.

● There is a flexible use of support aimed to promote joining in and inclusion rather than to create barriers and exclusion.

Getting started

In an inclusive approach, your task becomes one of making the National Curriculum accessible to all. The management guide, *Including All Children in the Literacy Hour and Daily Mathematics Lesson* (DfES) provides suggestions and advice on how you can cater for pupils with particular needs including SEN and how best to use classroom assistants. If you combine that general guidance with the tips in this handbook, you will have a starting point for addressing and meeting the needs of most SEN you are likely to come across in your class. Your role is not to *solve* special educational needs, but to *identify them, plan for them and meet them*. If you find that the child is still not making reasonable progress despite your interventions, then you can consult the SENCO and make use of the SEN framework with the Code of Practice.

Working with parents and carers

Parents and carers of children with SEN now have stronger rights and more choices. They must be involved and consulted throughout the SEN process. Most LEAs appoint parent partnership officers to offer advice and support parents at any stage of the SEN process. These professionals work alongside schools and support services but are also able to give independent advice. They can listen to parents'/carers' concerns and help them have their say or develop their input. You will find more ideas for working with parents and carers in Chapter 7.

INCLUSION

Where inclusion is working well, all children participate fully in all of the regular routines and activities of the school day. Here are suggestions for ensuring that this happens and that your school is as welcoming an environment as possible.

What do we mean by 'inclusive' education?

'Inclusion' is the practice of including all children together in a school. In fact, inclusion goes far wider than your school and is a philosophy that embraces the whole community and all of society. This becomes clearer if you read the Index for Inclusion on page 12. Over the past 35 years, we have travelled an exciting journey:

● from a starting point where many children with SEN were segregated or did not receive any education at all (before 1972)

● through a stage where these children were 'ascertained' as having difficulties and were educated in special schools

● through the point where they were integrated into mainstream schools 'if they could cope'

● up to the current time, where most are educated alongside all children by right and entitlement.

We are still on this journey: some of us are new arrivals, and others of us are still thinking about how we can work towards more inclusion for the families we serve. It is clear that schools need resources and support to develop the new skills needed and these still have to be developed in some areas. There may be certain children whose needs are so complex or severe that specialist placement will always be needed, but we can expect the number of these children to dwindle over the next decade as we become better resourced within the community and more inclusive in our approaches. The Government's strategy for SEN 'Removing Barriers to Achievement' shows how the various initiatives for inclusion are coming together so that professionals, parents, carers and children can work together to learn and succeed.

Planning for inclusion

Here are some practical ways in which you can encourage making learning approaches accessible for *all* children wherever possible.

● Try not to have 'special' activities for 'special' children or to buy more 'special needs' equipment than necessary, as this does not help the development of an inclusive provision. Instead, look for ways of adapting a whole lesson so that it is accessible to all individuals at various levels. In the activity books in this series, you will find ideas for lessons and activities which will serve as a starting point for planning inclusively.

● A lesson can often be changed in some way rather than excluding certain children because they cannot 'fit in' with it. Flexible approaches and adaptable timetables and routines will all make this easier.

● Outdoor play areas need to contain quiet, sheltered spaces as well as busy active areas. They should also provide some focused activities for children who have difficulty coping with an unstructured social environment.

● Indoors, tables and equipment need to be at adjustable heights, and floor spaces should be comfortable and safe to work on. Acoustics can be softened with soft surfaces, cushions, carpets and curtains, making it easier for everyone to hear clearly.

● Story and discussion times can be kept concrete by using props and visual aids.

● Communication can be enhanced by making sure that all adults are familiar with any language or communication system used by the children.

● Children with more severe learning difficulties can have a communication book of photographs and interpretations showing how they make their needs known (for example, 'This is Georgia when she is uncertain of something').

● Make more use of colours, textures and smells to encourage different senses and to develop sensory learning.

● Plan lessons that appeal to different learning styles and that include a mixture of listening, looking and doing.

● Consider ways of making tools and equipment easy to handle by all children. Here are some examples:
   – wrap foam padding around paintbrushes to make them easier to hold
   – try non-slip mats to hold small objects in position
   – adapt by providing tilted work surfaces for children with physical or visual difficulties
   – offer a choice of squeezy or left-handed scissors
   – collect a range of pencil grips
   – obtain adapted computer mouse or switch equipment
   – look for suitable IT equipment to meet a range of needs.

● Throughout the curriculum, look out for materials, illustrations and books that portray positive images of disabled people and special needs. You will find useful contact addresses on page 94.

Including all children

The DfES has produced guidelines on how to include all children in the Literacy Hour and Daily Mathematics Lesson and thus make the National Literacy and Numeracy Strategies (NLS and NNS) more accessible (details on page 94). There will be copies in your school held by the head teacher, SENCO, literacy and mathematics co-ordinators. The guidelines have detailed information about how to plan provision in literacy and mathematics for children who have SEN, how to choose appropriate learning objectives, how to plan strategies for enabling children with different learning styles to access the curriculum, and how to see all of this through into planning units of work in the Literacy Hour and Daily Mathematics Lesson. The 'graduated response' recommended in the SEN Code of Practice can be mapped on to the NLS/NNS Three-wave Framework in this way:

Wave One: the effective inclusion of all the children in a quality Daily Mathematics Lesson and Literacy Hour

Wave Two: small group interventions for children who should be expected to 'catch up' with their peers, given this extra support

Wave Three: additional and different approaches under the SEN Code of Practice.

In Wave Three, you might feel that it is not in a child's best interests to work on the same activities and objectives as the class as a whole. These are the children who have SEN and for whom you might need to 'track back' to a more elementary programme of objectives, either at an earlier level of the National Curriculum or on

to the QCA P Scales, which describe children's achievements at each of eight pre-National Curriculum levels. The document 'Including All Children in the Literacy Hour and Daily Mathematics Lesson' gives you guidance for tracking back through the Frameworks and, as such, should be an essential read for all teachers. The SENCO should be able to support colleagues through this approach.

You will find the two-week planning sheets particularly helpful since they enable you to visualise 'real' children and 'real' needs in a classroom context, with practical suggestions for progression and also what to do if a particular suggestion did not work. For those of us who learn by visualising and doing, as well as by reading, these kinds of example are invaluable and will help you to see that you already have many special skills to call on when planning for children with SEN.

The Index for Inclusion

Following the UNESCO conference in Salamanca in 1994, which advocated inclusion in education, an 'Index for Inclusion' team of teachers, parents, governors, researchers and a representative of disability groups developed a programme of research and trials in English schools. This led to the development of an 'Index for Inclusion' built on existing good practice and on ideas from other countries. The Index allows schools to travel through a process in which they consider how they perform at present, and how they might like to perform in the future in order to be more inclusive. It is an aid to reflecting on inclusion and on considering how to develop inclusive practices, policies and cultures starting from 'where you are' at present. The final version (see page 95 for details) was distributed free to all primary, secondary and special schools and LEAs in England.

You can use the Index in a variety of ways to help promote greater reflection about inclusion and lead to greater participation of children in the cultures, curricula and communities of their settings. Overleaf are some examples of what such an index might look like for your school.

Our organisation
● Our school welcomes all children from its local community.
● We work together to plan and deliver the National Curriculum.
● We support each other in dealing with difficulties.
● Any support assistants work with all the children.
● Parents/carers are partners in their child's learning.
● Our school seeks to enrol an increasingly diverse population.

Our social climate
● New children are offered particular support and encouragement.
● All children feel equally valued and respected.
● All children are encouraged to work and play together.
● Each child knows what to do if they feel in need of help or comfort.
● We tackle challenging behaviour by using positive teaching.
● Exclusion from and within our school is minimised.

Our communication
● We all take part in major decision-making.
● Everybody's views are listened to.
● We listen to the children's views and give them real choices.
● We keep parents and governors well informed about our policies and practices.
● Our school is well thought of in our local community.

Our relationships
● There is a sense of teamwork amongst staff.
● The children approach us readily for help.
● The adults are helpful and supportive to one another.
● We address each other in ways that confirm our value of each other as individuals.
● Our external support services support us in our efforts to increase the children's participation.
● Our visitors always feel welcome.

The experiences we offer
● Each child is entitled to take part in everything we offer.
● Teaching and learning are planned with all the children in mind.
● Our curriculum develops understanding and respect for differences and for different cultures.
● Each child experiences success in their learning and daily school lives.
● We use child-centred assessment methods.
● Difficulties in learning are seen as opportunities for developing our practice further.

Adapted from 'The Index for Inclusion' (see page 95).

Ensuring equal opportunities
The Disability Discrimination Act 1995 (DDA) brought in new legal measures to clarify disabled people's rights and ensure that they have equal opportunities. The Act was amended to cover the requirements on educational establishments, and this formed the Special Educational Needs and Disability Act (SENDA) 2001.

● Under the Act, a disabled person has 'a physical or mental impairment, which has an effect on his or her ability to carry out normal day-to-day activities. That effect must be substantial (not trivial or minor), adverse and long-term'.

● Most children who are disabled will have SEN and most children who have SEN are likely to be disabled in some way, so there is considerable overlap.

● Schools are required to overcome physical features which impede access to a service and from 2004 may have to make other *reasonable adjustments* to the physical environment to overcome physical barriers to access.

● You cannot refuse a service (such as education), offer a worse

standard of service or offer a service on worse terms to a disabled child or person unless you can offer a 'justification'. This is called the 'less favourable treatment' duty.

● You will be expected to demonstrate that you are planning ahead to improve access and inclusion in the future.

● Staff need to plan 'reasonable adjustments' for disabled children. This might include training for personal support assistants, planning accessible activities in an accessible environment, flexibility in terms of toilet arrangements and the provision of flexible transport. It would also include writing effective and inclusive individual education plans for those children who have SEN (Chapter 3).

The Act has still to be fleshed out as cases begin to come to court for judgement. You can therefore expect more Government circulars with guidance and advice over the next few years.

The special needs policy

All schools now have a SEN policy as a requirement of OFSTED inspection. If you are new to a school, you will need to read through this, so that you can understand how the SEN procedures operate in your school and how the SENCO can support you. The policy usually begins with a short summary of the beliefs shared by staff regarding children who have SEN. It might, for example, say that all children should be entitled to a broad, balanced and purposeful curriculum and that you will all work with parents, carers and other agencies to achieve this. It will then continue with the following kind of information:

● how the policy is to be achieved in your school

● how it is decided which children need help and what will be done about it

● how the children's progress is monitored and evaluated

● how staff members identify, intervene for and review SEN

● how additional resources are provided for children with SEN

● admissions arrangements with relation to children who have SEN

● how complaints about SEN provision are considered in the school

● the name of the school's SENCO with responsibility for the day-to-day operation of the SEN policy

● a list of staff with SEN expertise and qualifications and any specialist resources within the school

● who the local support services are and how these are accessed.

The role of the SENCO

The main responsibility of the school's SENCO is for the everyday operation of SEN policy and this might include:

● making sure that each class teacher sets up appropriate procedures for working with and including disabled children and those with other forms of SEN

● working with governors, staff and parents or carers on producing and reviewing a written SEN policy

● co-ordinating provision for children with SEN within their school and making sure that each child's SEN are being met

● ensuring that the needs of disabled children and those with other

forms of SEN are being included in all aspects of the school's planning and practice

● making sure that all staff understand the school's practice in relation to disabled children and those with other forms of SEN, and that there is consistency and continuity in the way it is carried out

● supporting staff in making observations and setting appropriate targets to meet individual children's needs and entitlements by ensuring that appropriate IEPs are in place

● contributing to statutory assessments and reviews for children who have statements.

SENCOs also have an important role in developing and maintaining positive relationships in order to ensure effective liaison with parents or carers. The SENCO usually takes responsibility for the school's liaison with external support agencies to gain information, advice or support in relation to particular children with SEN and on disability and SEN issues in general.

Supporting each other

Though the SENCO has the day-to-day responsibility for making sure that the SEN policy is implemented within the school, it is each teacher's responsibility to meet the SEN within their class. One way in which the SENCO and staff can support each other, solve problems and generate approaches and strategies for SEN is to use a consultative approach. This approach is often used by support professionals (such as educational psychologists) working with the school. It can also be adapted for SENCOs to use with staff.

Consultation

This is an exploration of a learning difficulty or concern leading to an approach for helping. A regular slot could be held each week in which you or the SENCO meet with staff to explore any concerns or difficulties with the children's learning or behaviour. The aim is for you to explore a concern and reach a better understanding of what is going on using joint problem-solving. This should help you all to work out more effective approaches and strategies.

Here are some ideas for planning a SEN consultation:

● agree a time limit to discuss each child – perhaps 15 or 30 minutes

● find a quiet area where you will not be disturbed

● make sure that you have arranged a time when those members of staff who know the child best will be present

● use photocopiable page 15 to direct the discussion.

● keep a record of the discussion – this may become part of your evidence for monitoring any SEN in the future

● Arrange to meet up again in three weeks to review progress and decide on what your next steps will be. You can use the photocopiable sheet on page 16 for this.

When you decide what you will do next, one of the options would be to involve parents or carers more fully and see if this makes a difference, or to plan approaches which are 'additional' or 'different' under the SEN Code of Practice. You will read about this in more detail in the next few chapters.

SEN consultation

Name of child:
Date of consultation:
Who was present?
What is the learning or behaviour you are concerned about?
What concerns you about this child's progress?
What approaches have you tried so far?
What effects have you noticed?
How would you like things to change?
Are there other factors you think might be important?
How are parents or carers involved?
What do parents or carers feel about the situation?
Is any other agency involved?
What will we do next? **Actions:**   **To be carried out by:**
When will we talk about this again?

Consultation follow-up

Name of child:	
Date of follow-up:	
Who was present?	
What was the original cause for concern?	
Progress made since we last met:	
How did our approaches work?	
What are our current concerns?	
What will we do next?	
Do we need to meet again?	

ASSESSING SPECIAL EDUCATIONAL NEEDS

It is important to find out about every child's strengths and weaknesses in order to plan appropriate interventions. This chapter has suggestions for assessing SEN.

The importance of early identification

The SEN Code of Practice tells us that we must identify pupils who may have SEN at the earliest possible time so that we can plan interventions. We know from a large body of research that early intervention can make an enormous difference to the future progress of children who are vulnerable to SEN.

Early intervention typically has these main goals:
● to help teachers and families provide the right kind of support to encourage their children's development and learning
● to enable each child to progress successfully by using a knowledge of individual strengths and weaknesses
● to help children to cope better emotionally with their learning
● to prevent future problems developing.

If an intervention for a child with SEN is to be effective, it should be designed with a clear purpose. It should provide as close a match as possible between the special educational needs that you have identified and the course of action that you will take in order to meet those needs. In this chapter, you will read about identifying and assessing any special educational needs in the pupils you teach. In Chapters 3 to 5, you will read about the interventions that you can design and the methods you should use to monitor them.

How do I know if a child has SEN?

Perhaps you are wondering for the first time whether a child has special educational needs that you ought to be addressing. It makes sense to allow the child time to settle in your class (usually for at least half a term) so that you can be sure that their needs do not respond satisfactorily to your usual methods of differentiation. This does not mean that you will be doing nothing about their needs in the meantime. You will be constantly observing and recording their progress and trying various approaches to help the child concentrate better, learn new ways of playing and behaving, or to communicate more clearly. But these approaches will be part and parcel of *what you would do anyway* for any child who is new to your kind of teaching and learning and who needs support to settle and begin to make progress.

There might come a time when you have tried all your usual approaches and the child is still not making the progress you would expect from other children of their age and with their experiences. In these cases, it is useful for you to know the legal definitions of 'special educational needs' and 'learning difficulty' as provided in the 1996 Education Act (Section 312).

● Children are described as having 'special educational needs' if they have a 'learning difficulty' which needs 'special educational provision' to be made for them.

● Children have a 'learning difficulty' if they have a difficulty in learning that is significantly different from the majority of children of the same age, or have a disability which prevents or hinders them from making use of educational facilities of a kind usually provided for children of the same age in schools within the area of the LEA.

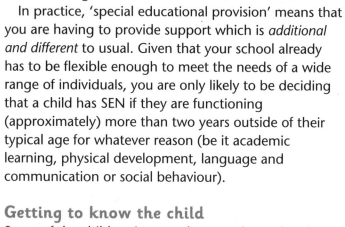

In practice, 'special educational provision' means that you are having to provide support which is *additional and different* to usual. Given that your school already has to be flexible enough to meet the needs of a wide range of individuals, you are only likely to be deciding that a child has SEN if they are functioning (approximately) more than two years outside of their typical age for whatever reason (be it academic learning, physical development, language and communication or social behaviour).

Getting to know the child

Some of the children in your class may have already been identified as having SEN in a previous school or class or by colleagues or outside professionals, and these children will therefore already be receiving support through School Action, School Action Plus or a statement of SEN (see Chapters 3 and 4). For other children, you may be identifying the child's SEN for the first time. Your first step will be to get to know the child well as an individual during their early days in your class. This cannot be a static process and will involve you interacting with that child in a variety of teaching and social situations, trying approaches and evaluating their success, as you would with each child in the class.

Getting to know the child also helps you to become sensitive to how they feel about their progress and any difficulties. You can then proceed carefully in a way that supports the child and helps them to feel successful rather than feeling singled out because they have (or, worse still, 'are') a problem. Being sensitive towards the feelings of the child when identifying SEN helps you make sure that self-esteem remains positive.

Initial concerns

While you are considering whether a child has SEN, it can be very helpful to have a system in place for recording your initial concerns. You will find a photocopiable example of an 'Initial concern form' on page 27 which you can use. There is an example of how to use the form on the right. At this stage, you will not have come to a conclusion about whether the child needs additional and different approaches and you will still be gathering information, putting your usual approaches into operation and beginning to assess how effective they are.

You can also use an initial concern form for recording temporary blips in progress. Perhaps a child is going through an unsettled time at home and their work is being affected for a while. Maybe a child is new to your class and you find that their literacy and numeracy skills are particularly weak. You are not sure how much this relates to lack of opportunity to learn or the newness of the situation (perhaps because of absences, changes of school or changes of teacher) and you might decide to use the initial concern form to record your plans and actions.

Here is an example of how you can use the form to register some of your concerns.

Initial concern form

Pupil's name: *Grant F*	Date of birth: *14.03.97 (age 8)*
Class teacher: *Geoff Thomas*	Class: *Y3*

Date: *May 3 2005*

My concerns:	My evidence:
Cognition and learning difficulties: (for example, general developmental delay, specific or general learning difficulties) *Grant has difficulty in reading and independent writing and spelling.*	* *SATs scores.* * *Vernon spelling age: 6:6 years.* * *Currently working at Y1/Y2 work.* * *Poor awareness of letter sounds and blends.*

Behavioural, emotional and social difficulties:
None — Grant tries hard.

Communication and interaction difficulties:
(for example, speech and language or autistic spectrum difficulties)
I am not sure whether he follows abstract vocabulary well — poor comprehension.

Sensory and physical difficulties:
(for example, physical and medical difficulties, hearing and visual impairment)
None — well co-ordinated.

How I am monitoring the concern:
* *Daily contact to celebrate progress and build up a folder of work he is proud of.*
* *Check weekly for retention of phonic skills and new spelling families.*
* *Evaluate progress 1 July.*

Gathering information

Gathering enough information to decide whether or not a child might have SEN should arise naturally out of the approaches you use to monitor the progress of all the children. This is the kind of questioning that you can use to decide whether additional and different approaches might be necessary. (See table on page 20.)

Cognition and learning

Is Callum more than a year behind what you would expect for his age? Is this despite his having had all the usual experiences to learn and despite your providing opportunities for learning familiar to his cultural context? (You might like to use the NLS/NNS Frameworks as a guide, tracking back in order to set and evaluate appropriate learning objectives for his age and stage.) What are his learning styles? What helps to maintain his concentration? What things motivate and stimulate him?

Communication and interaction

Can Stefan's spoken language only be understood by familiar adults in a familiar context? Is he mostly silent? Does he have difficulty in following a simple instruction in a familiar context? Does he find difficulty in socially interacting, even with an interested adult? Does he use only single words or learned phrases to express himself? Does he hardly ever respond to adult suggestion when learning? How does he make his needs known? What can adults do to help him understand more clearly? Does he receive help for a speech, language or communication difficulty? What approaches have helped? Is it necessary to incorporate any outside therapy and advice into an individual education plan to ensure adequate progress at school?

Behaviour, emotional and social development

Is Caitlin's behaviour extremely challenging both at home and at school? Once settled in, does she show no signs of responding to your class routines and rules; is this similar at home? Does she seem to be very unhappy, quiet and withdrawn, even once she has had a chance to settle in with familiar adults and familiar children? Are her parents concerned about her clinginess or withdrawal at home? What seems to help? Have there been major events in her life that she has had to cope with? Will she make a close attachment to a familiar adult in school? When is she most likely to do as she is asked? How seriously are other children affected by her behaviour?

Hearing

Has Ned had recurrent ear infections or colds in the past? Does his hearing go up and down? Has he failed two successive hearing tests? Has he seen a hearing specialist or had grommets inserted? Have his parents ever been worried that he is not hearing them? Does he have aids and how do these help? Do adults need to communicate with him in a particular way? How does he respond? Does he need additional and different approaches? Do you need specialist advice in order to be able to include him?

Vision

Can Ella see clearly, as far as you know? Has this been checked? Have her parents ever been concerned about her vision? Does she seem unable to make sense of what she sees (provide examples, such as being poor at reading or spelling)? How does she compensate for any difficulty? What approaches seem to help? Is your usual classroom differentiation sufficient to ensure adequate progress?

Physical development

Does Marc have a physical difficulty or disability that prevents him joining in the PE activities with the other children? How does this affect him? What resources, aids or methods of support help? Can he dress/ feed himself/go to the toilet unassisted? Where is he most vulnerable? What helps? Does he need different and additional approaches to be able to access the curriculum? Is he provided with opportunities to function independently from adults and to make close friendships with other children?

All these questions are merely starting points to finding out more about individual children's needs and how to meet them. You will find the other books in this series helpful for assessing and planning for particular areas of need.

Talking with parents and carers

An important source of information will be the parents or carers. Though they may not hold that information in a structured way that assists your teaching and planning, you can use your professional knowledge to plan the right questions and create a useful picture.

There are certain ways of questioning parents or carers which are constructive and productive and do not make them feel too defensive or dismayed. Questions need to be framed positively so that parents can tell you what their child can do, rather than supply a list of shortcomings. Make enquiries in a way that does not suggest a certain reply. Direct questions such as, 'Does she know her times tables yet?' can immediately suggest to a parent that perhaps their child ought to, and perhaps this will affect whether or not she will cope in class. However, questions phrased in terms of help are more positive, for example: 'How much help does she need when she is working with her times tables?' This leaves the parent free to proudly claim that their child is now proficient, or to talk openly about the level of help required.

This sort of open questioning can be used for many situations the child is likely to meet in the new class. Moreover, it supplies unbiased and practical information which will give much clearer evidence for additional support or resources than your school progress report alone.

If you decide that a child has SEN, then parents or carers must be informed. This is much easier if you have been gathering information and sharing progress (the triumphs as well as the shortfalls) from the start. While most parents/carers will be supportive of how you are trying to help, there will be others who ignore the situation, react emotionally, apply too much pressure on their child, or even become aggressive. You will read more about how you can adjust your approaches in Chapter 7.

Planning observations

Another powerful way of collecting information and evidence about individual children's learning is through observation. Observation is a method of finding out more about a child's learning or behaviour and it is most effective when you are clear in your mind *why* you are doing it. Possible reasons would include using observation as a means to answering a specific question such as, 'How long can Sula concentrate on a piece of written work?' or as a means of generating a hypothesis such as, 'Micky is swearing in assembly in order to draw attention to himself'. You can also use observation as a way to understand better a child's viewpoint, behaviour or feelings.

Your next question should be *what* to observe. This might be a child's gestures, language or body posture in a certain specific context. It might be a whole section of behaviour, such as a playtime or a numeracy lesson. It might be to observe the child's learning process during a certain activity, such as their reading strategy or their ability to calculate.

How you will carry out the observation will depend on the resources and time available to you. You might decide to keep a diary or biography of a child's learning or behaviour over a week. You might carry out a fly-on-the-wall observation of a PE lesson or assembly, writing down everything the child says or does in clear, unambiguous language. You might try a time-sampling approach when you observe the child briefly every 15 minutes to record any

difficulties or inappropriate behaviours. You might also keep a record of specific events, such as activities that went particularly well or badly for the child. You might have the luxury of an extra pair of eyes or hands so that you, or a colleague, can track the child through a number of different situations as they relate to different adults and different activities.

When you are carrying out an observation, allow yourself time afterwards to analyse the results and come up with a hypothesis or plan of action. Remember to try to see the situation from the point of view of the child and do your best to eliminate observer bias and subjective judgments.

Monitoring and review

It is helpful to have in mind a definite timescale after which you will review the situation and decide whether you are no longer concerned about that child's progress or you should be deciding that the child has SEN – perhaps a half-term. The SENCO can provide advice as to whether your concerns justify SEN approaches.

You might find it useful to have a summary sheet with all the children's names for whom you have initial concerns. This can be used to flag up review times and provide a running record of interventions and progress. There is a photocopiable sheet for you to adapt on page 28 and here is an example of what it might look like when completed.

Initial concerns summary

Name:	Date:	Areas to monitor:	Further action:	Review date:	Progress:
Callum	27 April	Concentration very poor, especially at group time. Needs prompting to follow instructions. Immature language though chatty.	Sit him near front. Use name and eye contact before addressing him.	10 May	Working much better in small group — keep going.
Emily	27 April	Spelling skills very weak. Cannot build or decode CVC words.	Check reading is being done at home. Use tactile letters to help word building. Move to blue group.	17 May	Still weak. We need to go right back to basics. SEN action.
Sultan	3 May	Attendance very poor. Low confidence. Bit of a loner. Check how good his English is.	Talk to Dad. Build confidence. Circle time.	24 May	Gradual progress. Continue with English support.
Lara	17 May	Very easily distracted. Looks unhappy. Gets very cross with us all.	See parents — is everything OK at home? Sit her next to Ellie for literacy work.	30 May	Family breakdown. Continue with extra support.
Jed	7 May	Poor balance and extremely clumsy.	Check pencil control. Observe in PE.	6 June	Need for structured handwriting programme. SEN action.

You will see from this that the teacher felt that two of the children would need additional and different approaches and she has suggested that Emily and Jed go on to receive SEN approaches. These are likely to be in the form of School Action (see Chapter 3) initially, perhaps moving to School Action Plus if outside advice and support becomes necessary. As English is not Sultan's first language, he continues to receive help through the LEA's multicultural service, though this is not considered to be a special educational need under the SEN Code of Practice. Callum continues to have difficulties with his attention, but these appear to be within the normal wide range for the class and so the general support continues. Lara is going through an unsettled time in her life and the teacher is expecting her to make progress again once life has settled down a bit. When the teacher looked more closely at Jed's co-ordination, she became more concerned rather than less, and decided that he too should be on School Action and have an individual education plan (IEP) to address his needs.

SEN assessment

Does an assessment of SEN need to be qualitatively different from the assessments used for all the children? In an inclusive approach, your assessment of SEN will arise naturally out of the observation and assessment methods you use for all the children following the National Curriculum. Each school needs to develop approaches and tools that can be used to identify a child's needs in their particular situation and these are recorded in the school's SEN policy and monitored by the SENCO. If an assessment is to work for your situation and for the child, then it has to be manageable and to be useful in planning. It also needs to be reliable and valid; in other words, it should not be based on 'assumptions' but on real 'evidence' of what children actually do that is observable by all who live and learn with them.

The SEN Code of Practice suggests that you make use of the following information when assessing the level of concern:
● the outcomes from any entry assessments or profiles
● the pupil's day-to-day progress against objectives in the National Literacy and Numeracy Frameworks, 'tracking back' if necessary
● the pupil's performance monitored by the teacher as part of the ongoing assessment and observation
● the pupil's performance against the level descriptions within the National Curriculum at the end of each key stage
● standardised screening or assessment tools if appropriate (you will find details of some suppliers on page 96).

At the end of the day, what you are doing is to make a comparison of that child's achievement, progress or behaviour with what you would expect from the rest of the class. If the difference is great enough, you will clearly need to provide additional or different approaches from the others. Again, the SENCO can provide advice as to what constitutes a great enough difference in your situation and what approaches you should be developing *anyway* to cater for a broad range of needs every day.

ASSESSING SPECIAL EDUCATIONAL NEEDS

You will find screening materials in the various programmes that have been included in the National Literacy and Numeracy Strategies, such as 'Early Literacy Support', 'Additional Literacy Support', 'Further Literacy Support' and the mathematical 'Springboard' series. These make the identification of SEN a more pragmatic approach – instead of having to spot 'something wrong within the child', you lean on your own expertise in teaching and identify those who are not likely to achieve the usual levels in the National Curriculum. All of this information is included in the document *Including All Children in the Literacy Hour and Daily Mathematics Lesson* (DfES).

What do I do now?

So far, you have recorded the fact that you have some initial concerns about a child's progress and you have gathered together all the observation and assessment information that you can. At what point do you decide that the child has SEN? The key test for whether or not further action is needed is whether you consider that the child is making adequate progress. You can never assume that all pupils will progress at the same rate and therefore you make that decision based on a careful assessment of the child's strengths and difficulties, the approaches that child seems to need in order to learn, and your school and class context. A judgement has to be made in each case as to what you feel it is reasonable to expect a particular child to achieve.

Take note of this dramatic shift from the way we used to regard special needs in former years. No longer are you required to be the SEN expert who can 'spot' difficulties within children, such as autistic spectrum disorder, dyslexia or dyspraxia. The child may or may not have this kind of diagnosis. Having SEN does not depend on having a medical label. Neither does it mean that, if a child *does* have a medical label, there will definitely be SEN. What you have to do instead is to take what action you need to in order *to ensure adequate progress*.

The *SEN Toolkit* (see page 94) provides guidelines on the strands of action you can take to meet a pupil's needs. These are backed up in the 'Wave' terminology of the NLS/NNS Frameworks (see page 11). You need to plan strands of action so that progressively more powerful interventions can be brought on board to meet increasing need. Even without resorting to SEN approaches, you can consider this kind of action:

● grouping the children differently, perhaps in smaller groups or setting different activities related to the learning objectives for the whole class

● using any additional human resources in a different way, perhaps as a 'shadow' in case of difficulty, as an extra supporter to a small group, or in order to release the class teacher to provide more structured teaching to a small group of individuals

● considering your curriculum and your teaching methods, making sure that you deliver the teaching in a way that suits the child's learning style.

There are practical examples of how this can be done at 'Wave One' and 'Wave Two' of the NLS/NNS in the document *Including All Children in the Literacy Hour and Daily Mathematics Lesson* (DfES).

By the same token, the range, type and intensity of interventions that you plan can be reduced or phased out as the child makes adequate progress – in otherwise planning interventions for individual needs is a two-directional process – you can phase out approaches as well as bring them on board. Children can, and do, make progress – interventions can manifestly work. For most pupils, differentiation at this kind of level will kick start progress and even help a child to catch up with the normal range of achievement shown by peers.

Where can I get support?

SENCOs should act as a contact for other members of staff on interpreting the Code of Practice and training. They should be able to support you in identifying and meeting the SEN of children within your class. In other words, they should help you work out which children's needs cannot be met through the differentiation and flexibility normally available in the class. The SENCO should oversee records kept on SEN for individual children. You will find it useful to build up a file on each individual child for whom you have concerns, with copies of any assessments, observations, interventions and plans, minutes of review meetings, parent letters and examples of the child's achievements and progress.

The SENCO should also be able to put colleagues in touch with relevant SEN training so that they can identify and plan for any SEN early. Schools still vary widely in the amount of protected time that is given to the SENCO to enable them to fulfil their role properly and to have sufficient time to train and support colleagues. Maintained schools have delegated budgets for SEN and it is becoming evident that giving protected time to the school SENCO can make an enormous difference to how well colleagues can plan for and support children with SEN. There is a move towards reducing the amount of funding that arrives via a statement of SEN (see page 55) attached to individual children towards delegating SEN funding to schools. This should make it possible to reduce the number of statemented children and plan for meeting needs more collectively and inclusively.

Triggers for planning SEN approaches

When you decide that a child has SEN, you have reached the stage where you feel you need more support and advice in the work you are doing with the child. You have realised that you might need to structure your approaches more carefully in order to provide those that are *additional* or *different*. At this stage, you would turn to the setting's SENCO and to the parents and begin to plan what School Action you are going to take together (see Chapter 3). Parents and carers should always be told when you are moving into SEN approaches and there is a sample letter that you might use for parents or carers on the following page.

ASSESSING SPECIAL EDUCATIONAL NEEDS

Dear

Now that I have had time to get to know _____ it would be helpful to meet up with you and talk about progress. This will help me to plan the best teaching approaches.

Please could you come into school on:
Date:
Time:
Place:

Do let me know if this time is suitable for you by sending in the reply below. If the time suggested is not convenient, please contact us to arrange an alternative appointment.

With thanks and best wishes.

Yours sincerely

I/we will/will not be able to attend the meeting on _____ to talk about the progress of my/our child.

Signed:

Name of child:_____ Class: _____

These are the possible triggers for planning School Action and deciding that SEN approaches are needed. Perhaps:
● the child has made little or no progress even when you have planned approaches which build on their strengths and support their weaknesses.
● the child shows signs of difficulty in developing literacy and numeracy skills despite small group work and targetted intervention.
● there are persistent behavioural, emotional or social difficulties that do not improve with the usual behaviour management approaches used by the school.
● the child has hearing, visual or physical difficulties that continue to pose barriers to the child despite the provision of specialist equipment, such as spectacles or aids.
● the child has communication or interaction difficulties and fails to make progress despite the provision of a differentiated curriculum.

It is no longer a requirement of the SEN Code of Practice that you should keep a SEN register as such, but you will need to develop your own systems within school for making sure that you maintain full records for each child with SEN. The next chapter covers what you can do once you have identified a child's SEN and will help you decide what information to record.

Initial concern form

Pupil's name:	Date of birth:
Class teacher:	Class:

Date:	

My concerns: Cognition and Learning difficulties (for example, general developmental delay, specific or general learning difficulties)	My evidence:
Behavioural, emotional and social difficulties:	
Communication and interaction difficulties: (for example, speech and language or autistic spectrum difficulties)	
Sensory and physical difficulties: (for example, physical and medical difficulties, hearing and visual impairment)	
How I am monitoring the concern:	

Initial concerns summary

Name:	Date:	Areas to monitor:	Further action:	Review date:	Progress:

SCHOOL ACTION

Once it has been decided that a child has SEN, then teachers should take School Action and plan additional and different approaches to support them. This chapter explains what each stage of the process involves for teachers.

The SEN Code of Practice

The SEN Code of Practice is a guide for school governors, SENCOs, school staff and local education authorities (LEAs) about the practical support they should give to children with special educational needs (SEN). Every school will have a copy (details on page 94), usually held by the SENCO. The Code gives guidance to schools, but it does not tell them what they must do in every case. Section 5 of the Code concentrates on the SEN action to be taken in primary schools. We will concentrate on how you can put this into practice and plan the necessary School Action in this chapter.

Following the Code

Instead of the five-stage approach of the old Code of Practice (Stages 1–5), the revised Code of Practice (DfES) has a graded approach to identifying and meeting SEN. This is in three phases: School Action (where the school assesses and meets the SEN),

School Action Plus (where you bring on board outside professional help) and statemented provision (where the LEA determines and monitors the SEN). Individual education plans (IEPs) should be a key feature of planning for any SEN in your class. The SENCO should help you to design and monitor these and will explain your duties to review these regularly. The SENCO should also be able to provide you with the general information, basic training and advice you need to meet your duties under the Code. You are not expected to be an expert straight away.

Inclusive provision

The revised Code of Practice also has a greater emphasis on inclusion for children with disabilities and SEN and this has been further strengthened by the SEN Disability Act (see page 12). You need to plan 'reasonable adjustments' for disabled children and, since many disabled children also have SEN, one of the main ways you can do this is to plan approaches that are *additional or different* to usual. This might include training for personal support assistants, planning accessible activities in an accessible environment, flexibility in terms of toilet arrangements and the provision of flexible transport. In your class, you will need to make sure that children who cannot walk or stand are not left out, by planning an alternative activity that includes all the children. Employ strategies for including all the children in group and circle time. If a child is non-verbal, look for alternative ways they can join in, answer the register and so on. You might decide to learn some basic sign language and share this knowledge with other staff and the children. The precise nature of your responsibilities under the Act has yet to be worked out through the legal system and the best advice is always to keep records that explain why you are making adjustments and how you are monitoring their effectiveness. In the meantime, you need to make sure that your admissions policy states that your school does not discriminate against disabled pupils in the education, day care or any other services it provides.

Gathering information

If a child is already known to have SEN, then gather as much information as you can before he or she joins your class. Many young children who have significant and long-term needs or disabilities will already have had these identified through their local child development centre or LEA support services. Others may be known to social services perhaps because they are 'looked after' by the local authority and have additional behavioural, emotional and social needs. They and their families will therefore have become known to some of the local support professionals. (The work of some of these professionals will be covered in more detail in Chapter 8.) As a result, there should already be a certain amount of information about a child's needs when they join the school. If the child has already attended another school or is joining you straight from a registered early years setting, the SENCO there should pass on information and records about their SEN planning for that child, showing you what has already been tried and how effective it was.

Parents and carers will also be a rich source of information about their child's needs. If a child with SEN is due to join your school and class, make a point of meeting with parents or carers beforehand to find out as much as you can. At this stage, you are entitled to be naive and to ask questions, so make the most of this window of opportunity. There are some exciting new national initiatives for building up parent-held records and using key workers to interpret the young disabled child's needs to others (for example 'Together from the Start' (DfES), see page 94). You are likely to come across

these in the next few years once the first pilot schemes have been evaluated and assessed.

Sometimes parents may seem defensive or anxious at their first meeting with you. Try to make sure you put yourself across as interested and positive, with the same goals as the parents/carers themselves – that is, to help their child be as successful as possible. Use open-ended questioning to find out how much support their child needs and what the likely barriers to learning or behaviour are likely to be. Find out who else is involved and clear any permissions (preferably in writing) to contact others outside the LEA for reports or information. The SENCO can support you in the gathering of this early information and in how to work out what the implications may be for the child and your teaching. Try to set some time aside during the child's first days with you to work alongside the child, establish a positive relationship and obtain a feel for how they are learning and behaving.

Keeping individual records

You will already be keeping information for all the children concerning the learning opportunities you have provided and each child's progress. What additional records do you need to keep for a child who has SEN? You no longer have to keep a SEN register, but you do need to maintain fuller records than you would for those children without SEN and so it makes sense to keep a separate list and file system. The pupil record or profile for a child who has SEN should include information about the child's progress and behaviour, from school, from parents or carers and from health and social services. What are the child's own perceptions of their difficulties? What strategies have been used to ensure that the child has access to the National Curriculum? How have these worked? What are the child's strengths and weaknesses? As you begin to plan approaches through a regular individual education plan, keep your records carefully together, adding your notes and monitoring sheets and records of reviews. These records might become important evidence if you feel you need to involve outside agencies at a later stage. They will show what you have tried and how effective your approaches have been over a period of time.

School Action

It is recognised that good practice can take many forms, and teachers are encouraged to adopt a flexible and a graduated response to the SEN of individual children. This approach recognises that there is a continuum of SEN. Some children's SEN will be met simply by your adapting your approaches and by targetting the learning more carefully. Others may require higher levels of support and differentiation and you might need to bring on board specialist expertise if the child is experiencing continuing difficulties.

Once a child's SEN have been identified, the providers should intervene through School Action. When reviewing the child's progress and the help they are receiving, the teachers (working alongside parents or carers) might decide to seek alternative approaches to learning through the support of the outside support services. These interventions are known as School Action Plus and are covered in the next chapter.

This does not mean that assessment should be seen as a linear process, moving from School Action to School Action Plus. Instead, assessment and intervention should be appropriate to a child's individual needs at any particular time, each review of the process informing and feeding on to the next. This graduated approach is firmly based within the school. Only a very few children will be considered by the LEA as having the kind of long-term needs that would benefit from a statutory assessment, perhaps leading to a statement of SEN (see page 55).

You need to have faith that the interventions you plan *can manifestly work*. Do not be tempted to feel that if you have identified a child's SEN then it requires a SEN expert to deal with them. Your expertise is delivering education and this is precisely what the child

needs. If you consider that about 20 per cent of all children will have SEN at some point in their school careers, ten to 15 per cent of all children will have their SEN monitored *within the school* without direct recourse to outside expertise (School Action). At any one time, a further three to nine per cent or so will have their needs met within school with the aid of outside professional advice (School Action Plus). Only one to three per cent of all children will need statements of SEN and an even smaller proportion (one per cent or less) will need special schooling. These figures have regional variations depending on how much support has been delegated from LEAs into schools and how many special schools have been maintained in that area. From 2003, schools were asked to identify in their annual returns which children had statements of

SEN and which were having their SEN met at School Action or School Action Plus. The idea is that the proportion of statemented pupils nationally will gradually decrease as local schools become more inclusive and better trained and resourced. While this is happening, education professionals are becoming more and more adept at identifying barriers to learning and planning to overcome them. School Action can and does work!

Planning an intervention

Having made a clear assessment, the SENCO and the class teacher will be in a position to consult with parents or carers and agree School Action. This is aimed at enabling the pupil with SEN to reach maximum potential and usually involves personalised teaching by

the practitioners and personalised learning on the part of the child. It will not always mean one-to-one teaching and, indeed, this might not be appropriate if the child is to be included fully in the curriculum. Staff should work closely with the child, following the plan that has been agreed, observing and recording the child's progress, and meeting with parents/carers and the SENCO to review progress. Parents/carers must always be kept fully informed of their child's progress.

The individual education plan

A feature of this individualised approach is the individual education plan (IEP). You should meet regularly with parents or carers to negotiate the IEP, twice a year or more frequently if you feel it is necessary. The plan should lead to the child making progress and should be seen as an integrated aspect of the curriculum planning for the whole class. It should only include that which is *additional to or different* from the differentiated curriculum that is in place for all the children. Differentiation of the activities planned (see page 63) will make the curriculum accessible to those children who have SEN. There are various ways of writing an IEP and practitioners need to develop a style that suits their situation and meets both legal requirements and the requirements they have themselves.

There is a photocopiable sheet for an individual education plan on page 42. In this pro forma, there is space for you to write three or four measurable and achievable targets in whichever strand of the National Curriculum you are concerned about. Your IEP should also contain information about the teaching strategies to be used to support the child, any additional provision you will put in place, how you will know whether or not you have been successful in your teaching and details of how and when you will review the IEP. In the example below, the class teacher has decided to design an IEP that is

Individual education plan – spring term

My name: Rufus   My birthday: 21.9.94   Class: 6T   My teacher: Mrs Taylor   Date: 12.1.05   School Action / ~~School Action Plus~~   IEP number: 5

My targets:	Activities:	Who will help me?	I will have achieved my target if…	Date achieved:
* To revise, read and spell words with soft c/hard c, soft g/hard g and other phonic props + learn class spellings. * To improve handwriting.	* Sound Activities worksheets * Starspell 2001/Wordshark * Spelling cards * 'Pages' word processing * Use handhugger, guidelines and Brain Gym Lazy 8s	Mrs Taylor Mr Benn	* I can recognise, read and spell 5 words from each group. * I can write joined script using a handhugger and form my letters correctly.	
* To read and spell correctly key sight words for story writing.	* Look-Say-Cover-Write-Check * Spelling games * Spelling sentences	Mrs Taylor Miss Soper	I can read and spell all 20 of the words when tested.	
* To improve my comprehension/handwriting and presentation.	Key Stage 2 literacy activity book	Mrs Taylor	I score 8/10 in class work.	
* To read at least 3 books. * To practise Brain Gym exercises.	* Words in reading book * Brain Buttons. Cross Crawling. Lazy 8s, Elephant 8s	Mrs Taylor Mrs Jones	* I can read my words quickly without hesitation. * I can do these exercises on my own.	

Signed by: Child _____   Parent/carer _____   Class teacher _____   SENCO _____

Date for review: March 2005

more child-centred so that she can share it easily with her pupils. On page 34 is what her completed IEP looked like for Rufus, a ten-year-old with specific learning difficulties. You will find references for some of the approaches she chose (the Starspell and Wordshark software and also the various Brain Gym activities) in the resources section. There is a blank pro forma that you can photocopy and use of this version on page 43.

Targets should be 'SMART' – specific, measurable, achievable, realistic and time bound, for example: 'By the end of this term, Rufus will be able to write joined script using his special pen and form all of his letters and joins correctly'. The IEP should underpin all your planning and intervention for the child with learning difficulties and should therefore always be shared with colleagues, parents and carers. It should always include *what* should be taught, *how* it should be taught and *how often* the additional or different provision is going be made.

The best IEPs will all have the following features:

- they are simple to manage
- they use clear and jargon-free language
- they raise the achievement of the pupil concerned
- they are specific and only detail what you are providing that is additional or different from the other children
- they also only include targets that are extra or different from the others
- they can be easily understood and followed by colleagues and also by parents or carers
- they are passed to all colleagues who need to know
- they help you plan effectively for all the class
- they result in successful interventions for the child concerned.

Group IEPs

Sometimes you might find yourself working with a group of pupils who have similar targets and common strategies. Your LEA support service might organise group tuition for pupils with literacy difficulties or you might have decided to group pupils with similar needs together and withdraw them for certain activities or lessons. In this case, you can draw up a group individual education plan rather than a series of individual IEPs. These can be shared and used in a similar way to the IEP, and pupils will benefit from having the opportunity to work in a group.

Group individual education plan

Year group: 2B	School Action/~~School Action Plus~~
Names of pupils: Ahmed Luke Kirsten	Dates of birth: 23.02.98 14.04.98 5.06.98

Shared difficulty:
Very short attention spans, poor looking and listening skills, weak literacy skills.

Targets for this term:
1 To sit and listen with interest to a ten-minute story and join in discussion afterwards.
2 To remember a three-part instruction.
3 To complete three sentences of writing independently.
4 To respond to group instructions.

Action:	Who by?
1 Withdraw group daily for 15 minutes during Literacy Hour, following NLS Framework.	Mrs C (classroom assistant)
2 Focus them by name before giving group instruction.	All of us
3 Use side table for written work.	Mr T (class teacher)
4 Daily memory games.	Mrs C

Help from parents/carers:
Memory games sheet to be sent home.

Monitoring and assessment arrangements:
Observations.

Review meeting with group of parents:
7 July, 3.30pm. With the opportunity for parents to talk to Mr T individually as well if they wish to.

Above is an example of a group IEP in which the class teacher is working with a group of three seven-year-old children who have very similar attention difficulties. There is a blank form that you can photocopy or adapt on page 44.

Regular reviews

The IEP needs to be reviewed regularly. Ideally, it should be under continuous review, though in practice, you are likely to set them over a fixed period and then review them formally. There is a photocopiable progress review form that you might like to use or adapt on page 45.

When you review an IEP, you should make an appointment to meet with parents and carers rather than fit it in 'on the hoof'. Though the meeting need not be highly formal, you do need to keep notes and circulate what you have all agreed afterwards. You might wish to plan one of the IEPs to coincide with a parents' evening, though you might find you need slightly longer than for the other children.

Your IEP review meeting should cover these points:
- the progress that the pupil has made since the last IEP
- what the current views of the parents or carers are
- what the pupil feels about the progress and support
- how effective the IEP was
- any barriers to the child's learning that need to be dealt with
- any new information or advice
- future action including the next IEP if you decide this is necessary.

If the child's progress remains adequate over a couple of reviews, you might decide together to lengthen the time between future reviews. You might also conclude that the child no longer needs additional or different approaches and that the IEP is no longer necessary. On the other hand, after several reviews, you might feel that a child is still not making the progress that might be possible. In this case, you might decide to call in an outside agency for some more advice, assessment and support. This is known as School Action Plus and will be covered in Chapter 4.

Who does what?

Here is a description of the main roles and responsibilities when a child's needs are being monitored through School Action. In the past, SENCOs tended to co-ordinate all SEN reviews and write the IEPs as well, but the move is now towards greater involvement of the class teacher, with support and advice from the SENCO. You may still find some variations in how the roles are divided in schools.

The class teacher

The teacher is the one who identifies the SEN in the first place through day-to-day classroom practice and observation. The teacher gathers assessment information on the child and informs the SENCO of the concerns and evidence for these. The teacher and SENCO then decide if that child has SEN and needs to be monitored through School Action. There is an 'SEN School Action summary' form that you can adapt or copy on page 46 and this can be used to keep a list of all the pupils in your class who are being supported through School Action.

It is usually the teacher who sends out a letter to parents or carers inviting them into school to share the initial concerns with teacher and the SENCO and to plan the best way forward (see page 26). Even if parents or carers do not attend, the teacher keeps them in touch with the School Action that is being proposed.

The teacher:
● decides and negotiates how best to bring parents and carers on board when making the individual education plan
● plans any subsequent IEP reviews until the child either no longer needs SEN approaches or until it is decided to move to School Action Plus
● organises the timetable so that the medium- and short-term planning for the class also includes the targets for the child with SEN
● organises class groupings and all available resources in order to provide the agreed interventions
● lets the SENCO know of any problems or difficulties that arise between reviews
● also makes sure that parents' and pupil's views are known regarding progress.

The SENCO

The SENCO, in turn:
● advises the class teacher on whether a child should be considered to have SEN, based on the concerns and evidence

● often contributes to the assessment of the child's needs in order to plan the best interventions
● decides on the format in which the SEN information on a child should be kept. This is often a simple ring-binder file containing all the assessments, observations, plans and reviews, parents' and child's views, photographs and records of their work
● helps the class teacher put together the IEP
● informs and advises parents and carers of the parent partnership services (see page 53)
● makes sure that parents and carers have copies of any reports, IEPs and decisions
● ensures that there are adequate resources in school for meeting the child's needs
● makes suggestions of possible approaches and resources that could be put in place for the child
● makes sure that the SEN policy for the school is being followed and that parents have a copy
● contacts outside agencies if it is felt that informal advice is needed at this stage
● takes the decision, along with teacher and parents, that the child no longer has SEN or needs to receive support through School Action or School Action Plus.

Parents and carers

Ideally, the parents and carers will also play a central role when School Action is being planned. They can supply information about their child's early development and progress. They may be able to provide the health record from the child's early years and their attendances at baby clinic. These will give you an idea of how the child achieved early milestones. You might find it helpful to ask parents about their child's hearing and vision or to find out about early language development.

Involve them in the child's IEP so that they play an active part in helping the child to achieve the targets. They will need to provide their consent if their child is to be monitored at School Action Plus and an outside professional asked to provide assessment and advice.

They should be encouraged to keep the class teacher in touch with any new developments or difficulties the child experiences at home.

They should attend all review meetings set at a mutually convenient time. You can adapt the invitation on page 40 and use photocopiable page 47 to involve parents or carers more fully prior to reviews. Use it either as a questionnaire to send home or go through it with parents as an interview or structured conversation.

Parents and carers should co-operate in home–school diaries and other home–school recording systems, though they may need encouragement and support to do so. Inclusive parent partnership means making sure that any language or translation needs are catered for.

Parents/carers should make sure that the child's basic needs are being met, that their child is encouraged and emotionally supported and that their child has sufficient sleep to benefit from your curriculum at school.

The pupil

The pupil should share the targets and be encouraged to add their own ideas or comments. There is a format that you can copy or adapt on page 48, which you can use to involve the pupil actively in their own review process.

The pupil should be invited to attend the IEP review, or perhaps be present at part of it if this is more appropriate. The child should be informed of the outcomes of the review, even if parents or carers have not been able to attend.

The child should also be given the chance for regular pastoral support so that any barriers to learning and progress (emotional or otherwise) can be identified and worked on quickly.

Drawing it all together

On the next page there is a checklist that should help you make sure that you have done everything you need to for a child who has SEN and whom you are supporting through School Action.

Dear

As you know, I have decided that it would be helpful for us to plan an individual approach for .... in order to help with progress. I am writing to explain what this actually means. When any children need an individual approach at school they are entitled to receive special educational needs (SEN) support. About a fifth of all children have this kind of support at some stage of school so it is not unusual. In your child's case, it has been decided to provide that support through School Action.

This means that the school will offer extra support and individual approaches for your child whose progress will be carefully watched for a while. An individual education plan has been put together detailing our targets for your child and how we hope to achieve these. I enclose a copy for you to keep at home. You will see that you are an important part of this plan and I look forward to working with you to help your child.

Please can you come into school when we review your child's progress on:

Date:

Time:

Place:

Do let me know as soon as you can if this is not possible for you. In the meantime, please do not hesitate to contact me if you have any concerns or questions about your child's progress.

Yours sincerely

● Have you given the child every opportunity to settle in and to respond to your usual approaches?

● Have you differentiated and delivered your curriculum to suit a range of learning styles and is the child *still* not making progress? If so, consider following SEN approaches.

● Have you carried out enough assessment and observation to convince yourself that this child needs additional and different approaches to the majority of other children their age? If so, follow SEN approaches and involve parents or carers at this stage.

● Have you shared your concerns with parents and carers and informed them that you are planning SEN approaches and explained what this means? You might find the sheet above helpful as a model for sharing this information.

● Have you gathered information about the child's strengths as well as weaknesses?

● Have you made a note of parents' or carers' views of their child's difficulties and tried to involve them fully in supporting their child's learning at home?

● Have you made an attempt to seek out the child's own perception of their difficulties and the help they would like?

- Have you set clear, crisp targets that are relevant and realistic for the child and teacher?
- Have you thought carefully about the implications for adult time, resources and equipment?
- Have you thought about how you will group the children and make best use of any classroom support?
- Have you drawn up an individual education plan and shared it with parents and carers?
- Have you involved the child in the target setting?
- Do all teachers who work with the child have access to the IEP?

- Do all teachers who work with the child have an understanding of the child's needs and how it affects their teaching situation?
- Are there common and consistent approaches for teaching style and for managing difficult behaviour with respect to that child?
- Is the IEP used to inform the curriculum planning for the whole class – that is, the child is included in the lessons but with a differentiated approach that ensures successful learning wherever possible? (There is more information about differentiation in Chapter 5.)
- Have you planned approaches that will support the child's confidence and self-esteem?
- Have you made a note of any pastoral or medical needs and what the implications of these may be for your teaching?
- Have you agreed on a review date with parents and carers?
- Have you kept them fully informed in writing even if they do not attend meetings?
- Have you thought about the role parents/carers and child will play in the review?
- Have you thought about how you will monitor the child's progress and how you will know when targets have been achieved?
- Have you been able to build in a mechanism of moving the child on earlier if the targets are achieved more quickly – for example, by using a method of continuous monitoring of progress where necessary, so you are always aware of what stage the child is at?
- When you meet to review progress, will you have evidence and examples of the child's progress to share?
- How will you pass on information smoothly to the next teacher or school at the end of the school year?

Individual education plan

Name:	School Action/School Action Plus
Date of birth:	Class:

Nature of difficulty:

Targets for this term:

1

2

3

4

Action:	Who by?

Help from parents/carers:

Pastoral or medical requirements:

Monitoring and assessment arrangements:

Review meeting with parents/carers:

Child's individual education plan

My name:

My birthday:

Class:

My teacher:

Date:

School Action/School Action Plus

IEP number:

My targets:	Activities:	Who will help me?	I will have achieved my target if...	Date achieved:

Date for review:

Signed by:

Child _____

Parent/carer _____

Class teacher _____

SENCO _____

Group individual education plan

Year group:	School Action/School Action Plus
Names of pupils:	Dates of birth:

Shared difficulty:

Targets for this term:

1

2

3

4

Action:	Who by?

Help from parents/carers:

Monitoring and assessment arrangements:

Review meeting with group of parents and carers:

Progress review:
School Action/School Action Plus

Name of child:
Date of review meeting:
Who was present?
Who has sent reports (attached)?
Progress since the last review:
Any special support arranged:
How helpful has this been?
Any recent changes in the situation?
Have the targets on the previous IEP been achieved? (Negotiate and attach the current IEP.)
Date of next review meeting:
This review report has been circulated to:

SEN School Action summary

Teacher:

Year group:

Name	Date of birth	Parents informed	Initial meeting	First review	Progress	Second review	Outcome

Parents'/carers' contribution to review meeting

Name of your child:
At home When does your child need most help at home? What does your child enjoy most at home?
About school Is your child happy to come to school? Are you worried about anything to do with school? How do you feel about your child's progress? Do you feel your child's needs are being met?
Health How has your child's health been lately? Have there been changes in any medication or treatment?
The future What would you like to see your child learning to do next? Are you worried about anything in the future? What questions would you like to ask at the review? What changes would you like to see following the review?

Child's contribution to review

My name:

The best thing that happened at school this term was:

The worst thing that happened at school this term was:

These were my targets for this term:

1

2

3

4

How well have I done?

1

2

3

4

I need more help to do these things:

These are things that worry me:

SCHOOL ACTION PLUS AND BEYOND

Some of the children in your school may require additional outside help. This chapter explains what support you can expect and how you can access it, as well as describing your role in the process.

School Action Plus

In the last chapter, we looked at how you can address the special educational needs of children by planning School Action. Some children with SEN require higher levels of support and differentiation and you might need to bring on board specialist expertise if the child is experiencing continuing difficulties – in other words, through planning School Action Plus. The specialist advice might come from an educational psychologist, learning or behaviour support teacher, speech and language therapist or others, and you will read in Chapter 8 about the various roles of these professionals and how they might support you. Who is actually involved and the kinds of advice available will vary with local policies and practices. You should find that the amount of outside support available to you improves as new national initiatives for supporting inclusion come into play.

Sometimes it is tempting to think of SEN assessment as a linear process, moving from School Action to School Action Plus if the child and the difficulty are not 'fixed' in some way. This should never be the case and you should plan assessment and intervention appropriate to a child's individual needs at any particular time, each review of the process informing and feeding on to the next. In other words, a child who needs a certain level of differentiation and small group work might continue to need just that and no more. Just because that child is not learning as quickly as the others need not mean that you have failed in your approaches and that you should call in the specialist or request a statutory assessment leading to a possible statement. Children who have SEN do not have a defect that you are responsible for curing. Instead, you are responsible for getting to know the individual needs of each pupil and planning accordingly so that you remove barriers to their learning and they can make the best possible progress. This approach embraces what is known as a social model of disability and SEN, rather than a medical model. In practice, you might feel after several reviews that a child is still not making the progress that might be possible for them. In this case, you might decide to call in an outside agency for more advice, assessment and support. The advice from the outside professional would then become part of the IEP (see page 33).

Seeking support

What happens if you have been taking School Action for a child who has SEN, and you still feel that they are not making the progress they might, even after you have taken advice and support from the SENCO? Perhaps you have planned approaches and monitored these with parents/carers over several review periods, but the child is not achieving the targets you have set. You should first revisit the targets you have put in place and make sure that you have broken them down sufficiently for the child to make progress. There are ideas in Chapter 5 for differentiating the curriculum and breaking steps down. For some children, you might find that you have exhausted your ideas and resources, and feel that the time has come to seek outside professional help. Parents or carers need to be in agreement, and this kind of decision would normally arise out of one of your regular review meetings. Usually, parents/carers are very happy to seek outside help if you put it to them that you yourselves need more advice and support in helping their child. Try not to give the message that you are asking for outside help in order to label their child or to confirm that their child is 'different' in some way. After all, about a fifth of all children are going to need individualised approaches at some stage of their school careers. You might find the standard letter below useful to adapt.

Dear

As you know, we have decided that it would be helpful for us to refer .... to an outside professional in order to help with progress. I am writing to explain what this actually means. In your child's case, a referral has been made to:

Name:

Title:

Address:

Telephone number:

When a school consults with an outside professional to plan suitable approaches for a child it is known as taking School Action Plus. This means that the school will continue to offer extra support and individual approaches for your child, but we will also be able to have the advice of a specialist to help us all.

The assessment/consultation will take place in school and we will let you know the date and the time and give you the opportunity to meet with the professional. Afterwards, you will be sent a copy of the report. Once we have the report, another individual education plan will be put together detailing our targets for your child and how we hope to achieve these.

In the meantime, please do not hesitate to contact me if you have any concerns or questions about your child's progress or the referral.

Yours sincerely

Usually, a request for help from outside agencies is likely to follow a decision taken by the SENCO, colleagues and parents/carers when reviewing a child's progress as part of School Action. You will be considering such questions as, 'Has progress been made?', 'What do parents feel?', 'Do we need more information and advice on the child's needs from outside?' The SENCO will be able to support you and make joint decisions in the action you take. The SENCO works closely with the teacher and draws on the advice from outside specialists in writing the new IEP. The SENCO must also ensure that the child and parents/carers are consulted and kept informed, though it is usually the class teacher who actually does this because of their close involvement. One of you (usually the class teacher) will need to make sure that the IEP (see page 33) incorporates the specialist advice, becomes part of the planning for the whole class and is reviewed regularly. The SENCO will also liaise with outside specialists, arrange for the child's progress to be monitored and reviewed and keep the head teacher informed.

Sometimes School Action Plus will lead to a special support teacher having input with the child. Your role might become one of co-ordinating their support so that the pupil is included in the curriculum. It is one thing for the child to learn a new skill in a one-to-one or small-group setting. It is quite another to learn how to generalise and consolidate that in a classroom situation. One without the other does not work, therefore, any individual or small-group work has to link closely to what is going on in class and, indeed, what can be supported at home.

Parents and carers should always be part of the decision to refer their child to an outside agency. In most cases, they need to give their express consent. If they are unhappy about this, explain that you wish to do everything that is best for their child and, to do this, *you yourself* need further advice from an outside professional.

Making a referral
The SENCO will arrange for a referral to be made to the outside professional, following the procedures for your LEA and with parents' or carers' permission. It is helpful to know what kind of evidence is requested by the LEA as part of the referral system, so that you can make sure that you collect it together consistently in the SEN dossier for the child. This evidence makes sure that outside support is targetted towards the neediest children and ensures that you have fully explored all the necessary avenues when taking School Action. To the referral, the SENCO will usually attach copies of:
- any assessments and observations that have been made
- the IEPs drawn up

- the review meetings you have held
- examples of the child's work or progress if appropriate.

At this stage, it is usually the SENCO who ensures that the child and parents/carers are consulted and kept informed about what appointments have been made and what plans agreed.

Requesting a statutory assessment

For a very few children (only about one to three per cent), the help

provided by School Action Plus will still not be sufficient to ensure satisfactory progress, even when it has run over several review periods. The provider, external professional and parents/carers may then decide to ask the LEA to consider carrying out a statutory assessment of the child's SEN.

In most LEAs, the SENCO consults a support teacher or educational psychologist from the LEA support services first, who will advise on completing the necessary forms and ensure that all the relevant evidence in support of a request is attached. A special form is usually needed and should be countersigned by parents or carers. Sometimes it is parents or carers themselves who write to the LEA and request them to consider initiating a statutory assessment. Parents/carers can seek further information about this from the LEA's parent partnership service if they need to (see page 53).

It is helpful if SENCOs once again attach evidence to any request to an LEA for statutory assessment:
- copies of IEPs
- evidence of the implementation of the IEP within the curriculum planning for the class and whether it was effective
- if relevant, a report concerning the child's general development and health, perhaps from the health visitor or school nurse
- the notes from review meetings
- reports from any outside specialists
- any written views of the parents or carers
- the views of the child.

This is another reason why compiling your evidence of the child's needs in the earlier phases of initial concern is so important. The LEA needs all of this evidence in order to make sure that the child's needs are indeed significant and have lasted, *despite appropriate interventions having been taken*. This decision cannot be made 'in a vacuum' (without a history and a context). Neither can it be made on the basis of a label or diagnosis (such as autism or AD/HD) without reference to how that condition is actually affecting the child's learning. In practice, you may have several children who are receiving support through School Action Plus. The summary form on page 62 should help you keep tabs on your reviews.

Statutory assessment

The LEA must decide quickly whether or not it has the evidence to indicate that a statutory assessment is necessary for a child. Parents/carers and professionals will probably receive letters from the LEA asking for their views on whether or not a statutory assessment should be made. If the LEA decides that it does not have enough evidence, then someone will write to you explaining why a statutory assessment has not been initiated. Do not feel too despondent if your request has been turned down. It might be simply because you have not provided sufficient evidence or that the funding needed has already been delegated to the school. Make sure that the LEA has sight of all your planning, seeking advice from the support services if you feel that your planning was not targeted carefully enough. If you are still concerned after another review period and you think that a statutory assessment should be considered, then you can apply again.

If the LEA decides to proceed with a statutory assessment, then it is responsible for co-ordinating this. It will call for the various reports that it requires, from a teacher (usually the class teacher or SENCO), an educational psychologist, a doctor, and the social services department if involved, and will ask parents or carers to submit their own views and evidence. The doctor (usually a school doctor or community paediatrician) collects together any reports and evidence from other health service professionals involved such as a speech and language therapist, occupational therapist or physiotherapist.

Supporting parents/carers

Over this time, parents/carers will receive a number of formal letters from the LEA. These can be rather daunting, but the LEA is required by law to send them. It is often helpful if you can reassure parents/carers about their contents and put them in touch with an independent parental supporter or parent partnership officer if they need explanations or have concerns or queries. A phone call to your LEA will inform you of the names of the IPS and PPO for your area.

An independent parental supporter is somebody who can support parents/carers through their child's statutory assessment and afterwards. When the LEA starts a statutory assessment, it must inform the parents/carers of someone who can give advice and information as well as telling them the name of the 'named officer' of the LEA from whom further information can be obtained. LEAs also appoint parent partnership officers who can put parents/carers in touch with this kind of support.

It may also be possible for a parent/carer to be introduced to an independent parental supporter through a support group or local volunteer centre. Many of these independent parental supporters are themselves parents or carers of children with special needs who have volunteered to support other families. Some parents/carers may feel that they do not need an independent parental supporter. If this is the case, many LEAs will give the name of local and national support groups and the parent partnership officer should be available for as long as the parents/carers wish.

What happens next?

The statutory assessment follows strict time guidelines, and when the school is approached for a report, a precise time for returning it to the LEA will be given. The whole procedure must not take longer than six months unless there are exceptional circumstances, which are defined clearly in the full text of the Code of Practice. Your role becomes one of continuing to meet and monitor the child's needs in the interim, of helping support the parents/carers through the process where appropriate, and submitting any useful assessment information when you are asked to.

You will need to gather all the assessment information you have for the child. You are in a unique position to provide information about how the child is learning and developing over a continuous period of time. Only you can provide evidence of where the child is learning within your curriculum and of what approaches have proved problematic or effective. You will probably be asked to submit a report directly to the LEA, and, if so, you will be told if a particular form is necessary. Sometimes this form is known as 'Appendix B: Educational Advice' (see page 56) since it can later form one of the appendices to any statement of SEN that the LEA decides to write.

Writing a report

The fact that your report forms part of a legal process might seem daunting, but all the information should be readily available in your existing records. You will already have saved copies of your IEPs and reviews so that you know what interventions have been tried and how effective these were. You will have gathered evidence of all the

children's progress over time and probably have done so in far more detail for any child with SEN. You will also have kept records of any advice received from health and social services and so will be able to show how this was included in the personalised approaches for the child. You will have records of SATs and other assessments and you will know which levels of the National Curriculum the child is learning at. Only you, the class teacher, will know how the child is actually learning and progressing through the curriculum, what the particular strengths and weaknesses are and how the child responds to support. Only you can write a 'pen picture' of that child in school, thereby getting across to others who must administer the information how the child presents in a day-to-day situation. Aim to portray the 'essence' of the child to those who might not know him or her. Remember that your report will be copied to parents, carers and all others involved. Make sure that you have objective evidence for what you say and take time to talk it through with parents and carers before sending it in to the LEA.

Overleaf is an example of some notes by a Year 5 teacher, Mrs H., when she was preparing to write an 'Appendix B: Educational Advice' form about George, a pupil with learning difficulties.

Statements of SEN

The statutory assessment may or may not lead to a statement of special educational needs. When it has gathered all the evidence, the LEA might feel that a statement is necessary because of the special educational provision required. Parents/carers have various rights of appeal to a SEN Tribunal if they are not happy with the statutory assessment procedures, and these are also fully covered in the SEN Code of Practice. The independent parental supporter can advise parents on their rights and choices.

A statement of SEN states what the child's special needs are, what provision will be made, how the needs will be monitored, and where the child will be placed. It is the responsibility of the LEA to name the school that the child should attend, taking parents'/carers' views into account. Sometimes, an LEA decides that there is not sufficient evidence for a statement and writes a 'note in lieu' instead. This is rather like a more formal IEP and is implemented and monitored by the school.

Including statemented children

If your school is named as the child's placement, then you will need to see a copy of the child's statement. This will set out what the child's special educational needs are, what should be done to meet them, what special educational provision will be made to do so, and what the monitoring and reviewing arrangements should be. Even though the child has a statement, it is still your role to continue to meet and monitor the child's special educational needs as you did before, though this will now be with the support and provision named on the statement. Usually this will involve regular contact with a member of the support services, who will be helping you to set the child's IEPs and to review progress. Sometimes, there is

additional equipment or perhaps additional hours of support provided to help the child in the setting or to aid staff with curriculum planning. However, if a child has a statement of SEN, it does not follow that there will be additional hours of support provided. It all depends on the child's needs and what the LEA decides is appropriate to meet those needs. Now that so much SEN funding has been delegated from LEAs to schools, most pupils who need only a certain proportion of additional support can access funding from their school's SEN budget. If a pupil has a very high level of needs (in some LEAs, this is pupils who require more than 20 hours per week of support assistance), funding or special school placement might come through the LEA. Even with the movement towards inclusion, it is usually recognised within LEAs that there will be a small proportion of children who have complex and multiple needs that might require placement within a special school in order to access the right amount of resources and therapy.

APPENDIX B
EDUCATIONAL ADVICE

Surname: *Dodds*   Other names: *George*

Date of birth: Home address:

School providing advice:

Description of the child's functioning (including strengths and weaknesses):
—Start with our context — size of class, open plan, staff ratios — get across the context in which G. is being taught.
• Describe G's current abilities — strengths as well as weaknesses:
  • Physical (no problems)
  • Emotional (very low confidence)
  • Cognitive (takes longer to learn than others and much repetition and consolidation needed — forgets day to day...)
  • Perceptual and motor skills (weak pencil control and clumsiness)
  • Adaptive skills (self help — still needs supervision)
  • Social skills and interaction (finds it hard to negotiate in the playground, loner, plays with youngest children)
  • Approach and attitude to learning (tends to just sit and stare unless I constantly chivvy and encourage him — visual and kinaesthetic learner)
  • Educational attainments (mention NC levels and recent group tests)
  • Self-image and interests (mention that wonderful Xmas play... his fishing... include his views of the help he wants)

• *Behaviour (borrow from our behaviour observations — include extracts perhaps to illustrate where we find his behaviour hard to manage)*
• *Then mention his home situation — choose words carefully... the particular challenges faced by his family — meet with G's dad to share the right wording perhaps?*
• *Must check: relevant aspects of G's history — look back into notes taken on entry to school — wasn't there something about an early hearing loss and an assessment at the Child Development Centre? (This will provide evidence that he has had his difficulties long-term.)*

Summary of the special educational provisions made so far for the child:
All this will be in SENCO file — simply write time log and summary and attach all IEPs, review notes and so on. Emphasise what worked and what didn't.

Aims of provision (for Cognitive, Physical, Social or Emotional development including teaching and learning approaches. This should contain reference to medium- and long-term objectives):
• *Check planning file for class and add what I would hope G. to achieve in a term's and a year's time, given the right support — for example, that he can cope with playtime independently, read at a KS2 level, write a short story independently — use NC Framework for inspiration?*

Special facilities or resources needed:
• *My realistic 'wish-list' for G. but everything must have evidence in what I said in (a) to (c)! Remember to identify sources of information.*
Summary:
• *Leave till end. Ask SENCO to help me. Avoid jargon, use clear wording and (however involved I might feel) avoid subjective descriptions and judgements!! Perhaps SENCO can check that I've been objective throughout — G. is very close to my heart!*

Signed: Position:

Countersigned: *Head teacher*   Date: *due in a fortnight*

The statement review
The LEA will ask the SENCO to call regular annual reviews to monitor whether the child's needs are being met. What does the SENCO need to do at this point?

● The SENCO needs to invite parents/carers and any support staff, community doctor, therapists or social worker involved with the child to attend the review.

● It is also helpful to invite any potential future school prior to possible transfer, especially for the review meeting before transfer to secondary school.

● The class teacher, any personal support assistant, and the SENCO should also be there to provide their input.

● Meetings should be called six weeks in advance, and all professionals involved should be invited to submit a written report if they feel it is appropriate.

● The SENCO needs to ask for these reports to be sent at least two weeks before the review so that they can be circulated in advance to everyone attending. (Not all professionals will actually produce a report, but the Code of Practice requires that they be invited to.)

● At the review meeting, a member of staff (usually the SENCO) will normally take the chair.

It is important that annual reviews are carried out effectively and that those who are involved are included. However, there is no value in including those who are not involved in the child's education and support. We can expect further guidelines in the future as review procedures are streamlined and as bureaucracy is decreased – in the meantime, the motto is keep it simple. Information should be gathered on a special review form and sent in to the LEA and all others involved in the review. Certain sections ask the question of whether the child still needs a statement, what changes in provision are suggested, and what are the main targets that the child should work towards over the next review period.

The review would normally be sent to the LEA with reports and IEPs attached. The LEA would then circulate it. It is likely that much of this kind of information will become electronic in the future saving much time and making it easier to share information

effectively yet respecting confidentiality where appropriate. There is a pro forma on page 47 for a parent/carer contribution to a review meeting which you can copy or adapt and on page 48 a possible format for involving the child's view.

Removing barriers to achievement

All children have the right to a good education and the opportunity to fulfil their potential, whatever their level of need. Nowadays, all teachers should expect to teach children with SEN and each school is required to play its part in educating children from the local community, whatever their ability or background. You will find that you are living in a time of revolution as far as meeting SEN is concerned, with a whole framework of guidance, support, training and new resources coming on board with the new Government initiative 'Removing Barriers to Achievement' (see page 94). The idea is that, as schools become better able to meet the needs of the children and to plan personalised learning for them, so parents and carers develop confidence that their children's needs will be met effectively in schools without the need for a statement. In time, as the skills and capacity of schools to meet diverse pupil needs improve, it is expected that only those with severe and complex needs, requiring support from more than one agency, will need the protection that a statement provides.

The social model of disability and SEN discussed earlier in this chapter encourages us to think not in terms of individual children's impairments so much as the barriers to their learning that exist. Difficulties in learning can arise from an unsuitable teaching

environment – perhaps pupils are grouped inappropriately, teaching styles are too inflexible, or curriculum materials are inaccessible to certain children. Children's emotional and mental health can have a significant impact on their learning and on their ability to make the most of their learning, as can family circumstances. Looking to the future, the trend will probably be that we meet more children's SEN as School Action and School Action Plus, rather than having to resort to statutory assessment and a statement of SEN. This will become possible as more resources are delegated and as support services become more accessible and 'joined up'.

Special schools

Children should be able to attend a local mainstream school wherever possible, and parents or carers should feel confident that this is the right choice. It works best when there is a successful partnership between the LEA, schools, health and social services and voluntary organisations, so that there is a network of support and communication. You will see a gradual change in the role of special schools as special education becomes more inclusive and fewer children are given segregated provision. Segregated provision is likely to be reserved for children who have multiple and complex needs that require more than one agency to support them.

There are plans to help special schools develop an outreach role so that expertise cab be shared between special and mainstream schools. Your LEA will keep you informed of these changes. You are likely to see:

● greater staff movement across special and mainstream sectors so that you can share expertise and experience

● more pupils able to move between the two sectors using annual reviews of their statements to plan the best balance

● more special schools involved in federation, cluster and twinning arrangements with mainstream schools

● more advice from special school teachers on how to asses and plan the curriculum for children who are working below level 1 and within the P Scales (see page 94).

Learning support assistants

Sometimes a child who is receiving support at School Action Plus or through a statement is given the opportunity to work with a teaching assistant or learning support assistant (LSA). These colleagues play a valuable role and can usually provide support to the child or a group of children for small-group activities or offer wider support in the classroom. Sometimes these assistants are asked to provide one-to-one support to a child with SEN. It is important that the teacher and LSA play complementary roles so that working with the does not deprive the child the opportunity of working with the other. It is also important to try to avoid the child becoming over-dependent on the LSA or on having one-to-one help. Make sure the child's IEP targets ways of supporting the child to learn within peer groups, so that the child develops more social and collaborative skills and becomes a more independent learner.

The role of the LSA will change depending on the individual needs of the pupils who are being supported.

● Where pupils have *physical difficulties*, such as cerebral palsy, the LSA's main aim will be to enable the pupils to be as independent as possible. They might need to carry out programmes of therapy under the guidance of a physiotherapist, speech and language therapist or occupational therapist. They might also be required to assist with mobility (for example helping with wheelchairs) to enable the children to get from A to B.

● Where children have *visual impairment*, LSAs are sometimes asked to enlarge worksheets in advance of activities, under the guidance of

a visiting teacher for visual impairment. If there is a practical demonstration taking place beyond the child's vision, they sometimes relay that information to the pupils. At other times, there might be close-circuit television available that the LSA will set up and operate in order to bring practical demonstrations 'nearer' for those who cannot see clearly. Sometimes, LSAs develop skills in Braille and are able to act as instructors.

● For children with *hearing impairment*, LSAs might be involved in relaying information to the pupil via a radio aid, or in teaching the child sign language. Sometimes they work under the guidance of a teacher or speech and language therapist to provide small group work aimed at filling the 'gaps' in a child's vocabulary and understanding of concepts.

● Where children have *speech, language and communication difficulties*, the LSA might be working with a group of pupils under the direction of a speech and language therapist or specialist language teacher. Sometimes, the LSA will act as an unobtrusive 'shadow' for children with autistic difficulties, stepping in to help the child with problem-solving, or assisting with transitions from one situation to another or unstructured situations such as break times.

● Children with severe *behaviour, emotional and social difficulties* sometimes need their LSA to serve as an attachment figure in order to help them become less anxious and more able to think clearly about controlling their own behaviour. Sometimes, the LSA can work with these children in a smaller group, making use of good role models from the other children and setting up the learning situation so that everyone achieves success. The LSA might also be asked to run a behaviour management programme, stepping in to a pre-agreed routine when certain behaviour is exhibited.

Learning Support Assistants can also play an invaluable role in preparing materials and resources for pupils with SEN. They can provide in-class support in order to release the teacher to work with an individual child for a short period, or deliver a differentiated curriculum to a group of pupils under the direction of and with the support of the teacher. Whatever individual or group support is available, it can never compensate for a curriculum that has been poorly differentiated and it is vital to consider differentiation as the first step to support. In the next chapter, you will read about ways in which the curriculum can be differentiated so that it is tailor-made to the needs of individual children.

School Action Plus summary

Year group:

Teacher:

Name	Date of birth	Name of outside professional	Referral date	Outcome	Date of first review	Progress	Date of second review	Outcome

DIFFERENTIATION

When inclusion works well, activities and lessons are changed in some way to make them accessible to all the pupils. This chapter deals with ways in which you can differentiate the curriculum, delivering personalised learning wherever possible.

Providing an inclusive and differentiated curriculum

When planning School Action and School Action Plus you are required not only to plan support for the child with SEN but to *differentiate* the curriculum in order to make it accessible for all. In this chapter, you will read some of the most familiar ways in which you can differentiate the curriculum you are offering. When planning differentiation, you have two useful strands of information to lean on and you will look at both in this chapter. One strand is the guidance that has come to you concerning national teaching strategies and the other is information that has developed historically from the SEN sector on how to break learning activities down into steps.

Recently, there has been a great deal of advice that has arisen from the National Literacy and Numeracy Strategies (NLS and NNS). You should have a copy in your school of the DfES guidelines on how to include all children in the Literacy Hour and Daily Mathematics Lesson (see page 94). These guidelines have detailed information about how to plan provision in literacy and mathematics for children who have a range of SEN, how to choose appropriate learning objectives, how to plan strategies for enabling children with different learning styles to access the curriculum and how to see all of this through into planning units of work in the Literacy Hour and Daily Mathematics Lesson. The advice brings together much of what we know about how to make inclusion work and how to take account of different teaching and learning styles. In Chapter 1, you considered how the 'graduated response' recommended in the SEN Code of Practice can be mapped on to the NLS/NNS Three-wave Framework in this way:

Wave One: the effective inclusion of all the children in a quality Daily Mathematics Lesson and Literacy Hour.
Wave Two: small group interventions for children who should be expected to 'catch up' with their peers, given this extra support.
Wave Three: additional and different approaches under the SEN Code of Practice.

Most of the time you will be teaching children within two years of the expected norm for any age (some may be a year or so ahead or a year or so behind and you would expect this). However, in Wave Three, you might find yourself 'tracking back' to more elementary objectives, either at an earlier level of the National Curriculum or on to the QCA P Scales, which describe children's achievements at each of eight pre-National Curriculum levels. The document *Including All Children in the Literacy Hour and Daily Mathematics Lesson* gives you guidance for tracking back through the Frameworks.

The P Scales

You will find details of these on page 94. You are likely to see greater use of these scales over the next few years as children with more significant and long-term SEN become included in their local schools. P Scales are already used widely in special schools and help teachers assess the progress made by pupils working towards level 1 of the National Curriculum. If you visit the DfES website from time to time (details also on page 94), you will be able to make use of the 'moderation' materials when they are published to help schools make judgements on a more consistent basis. From 2005, information on P Scale assessments is likely to be collected nationally so that comparisons can be made about pupils working below National Curriculum levels. There are also plans to develop new P Scales to assess pupils' broader achievements within the area of Personal and social development.

The curricular framework, therefore, provides your first tool for differentiation. Each and every child is a unique individual with specific learning needs and you can no longer expect children to fit the teaching. Instead, the teaching must fit the children and you have considerable guidance on how this can be done. The two-week planning sheets in the document *Including All Children in the Literacy Hour and Daily Mathematics Lesson* are really helpful in letting you see how individual planning can also fit comfortably into planning for the whole class. It is a skill that will take confidence and practice, but it is a skill worth learning and this is certainly the way that SEN teaching is going in the future. There are practical suggestions for progression and also what to do if a suggestion does not work. Since you should already have this document available in school, we will now look at the approaches that have come historically from the SEN sector and that can be usefully added to your 'tool box' of approaches for differentiation.

Personalising learning

The strategy for SEN 'Removing Barriers to Achievement' (see resources on page 94) emphasises the need for everyone to make education more responsive to individual children. This means delivering *personalised* learning and it involves:

● having high expectations for all children, with and without SEN
● building on the knowledge, interests and talents of each child
● making sure that children are involved in their own learning and share the objectives and the feedback regularly
● developing children's confidence in their own learning
● helping children to develop the skills they actually need once they leave school.

When you differentiate the curriculum, you are essentially breaking steps down or coming at the teaching in a different way in order to ensure a successful outcome. It is by succeeding that the child learns. In this way, you are, in effect, personalising the child's learning. Here are some ideas for doing this, this time based on individual teaching targets for a child with SEN rather than your teaching of the whole class (covered above).

Keeping it simple

The content of a source material or a comprehension text, for example, may need to be at a level appropriate to the child's stage of language. You might need to include props at discussion time in order to hold attention, emphasise meaning and allow a child to participate with more than one sense at once. You might find that you have to show the child what to do as well as tell, and simplify material to be learned or to produce highlighted summary sheets so that information can be more easily retained.

Allowing plenty of time

You might need to allow a child extra time to respond, or ensure that they sometimes have opportunities to 'get there first'. These are ways of building up their confidence. Instructions and demonstrations may need to be presented or repeated at a slower pace to certain children in order to ensure understanding. A succession of materials might be presented in order to maintain interest during a discussion. Some children need to sandwich short periods of structured writing activity with less structured or more informal activity. Some children take a long time to process information, and need longer silences than usual if they are to answer a question or fulfil a request. Others may find it hard to remember more than the last piece of information they were given, and therefore need supporting and prompting at each step, taking longer to carry out structured activities. Children with specific learning difficulties such as dyslexia and development co-ordination disorder (dyspraxia) may need longer to copy information down from the board or to record their homework.

Breaking it down

When you are planning your short-, medium- and long-term learning objectives, you are bound to be making allowances already for different levels of children's ability. Within this, some children might need the learning steps to be broken down further, and you may need to give value to a smaller and less obvious learning outcome for individual children. While you might expect one child to be able to write a page of imaginative story, you might expect another to draw a mind map of six good ideas and then form six simple sentences.

Making it possible

This involves the way in which materials and resources are presented. Some children with physical difficulties may need adapted scissors, tools or writing implements. Graphs and illustrations might need to be simplified, or some children might need table tops heights to be adjusted. Some might need radio hearing aids, or to sit close up to enlarged texts to see. Sloping desks place work at a suitable angle to make visibility better, or close-circuit television might be used to relay a practical demonstration to a child with visual impairment.

Using actions

Some children may be able to *show* they have learned through actions rather than words and any response that the child is able to give needs to be valued. Some children might rely on sign language to make their words clear. Others may not be able to tell you their wishes, but can demonstrate by their expressions, their choices or their behaviour what they would like to do next or where they feel confused. Some might find it hard to tell you what they like or dislike, but can be encouraged to point to smiley or sad faces as a non-verbal response.

Choosing your moment

Some children need to have opportunities provided at different times, or need to cover different aspects of a topic at separate sessions. If attention is short, it might be necessary to revisit an activity at another time in order to ensure success. Some children find it harder to settle and to concentrate after they have been very active. Others need to 'let off steam' for a while in order to return more attentively to an activity. If a child with behaviour, emotional and social difficulties is in the wrong frame of mind, you would avoid confrontation and wait for the right moment to make your requests or demands.

Thinking about structure

Some children learn best when they are learning in a highly structured setting, led and supported by an adult. Others seem to respond when provided with exploratory learning and supported in developing their own agendas. Every child needs opportunities to participate and to learn both on their own terms and in groups with other adults and children. Some children find unstructured situations, such as break times, particularly challenging and teachers have looked at ways of introducing structure through the different use of spaces and play equipment.

Giving more attention

Some children need more individual adult support and time. This can include some one-to-one work or withdrawal into a small group, but mainly refers to supporting the child with additional encouragement and prompting within the regular group. Simply having a heightened awareness of the child's individual needs can aid teacher involvement.

Using groups

The group structure may afford opportunities to allow the child to respond, or for other members of the group to provide good models which can reinforce the child's learning or behaviour. Sometimes meeting the needs of individual children with SEN has led to

children working alone on individual materials. This is not providing the child with an inclusive curriculum. Arrangements to include the child's individual education plan within planning for the *whole class* can overcome this and lead to a more purposeful and supportive way of meeting special needs.

Providing help

You can also provide different kinds and levels of adult help in order to make sure a child completes a play activity successfully. You might expect a child to get on socially with another child, but stay close to provide support. Perhaps you subtly direct a child to the correct choice when asking them to 'give me the one that is a cylinder'. You might use a gentle hand-over-hand prompt to guide them when they are pulling on their shoes, cutting with scissors or drawing a graph; or you use your words to guide or remind the child frequently – 'Hands on your knees', 'Please share the glue', 'Please look at me'. All these are different ways of using your help to make a task or activity easier for a child to succeed. You will read more ideas for prompting and helping later on in the next section.

These general approaches to differentiation are common sense and arise from your personal knowledge and experience of the child and their needs. Taking time in the early stages to closely observe and monitor the child can help you 'tune in' to the way in which children are experiencing their time with you and allow for more practical differentiation where opportunities are lacking.

Making steps smaller

The process of breaking down a teaching goal into several smaller steps or component skills is known as 'task analysis'. These steps bridge the child's present level of skill (sometimes called the 'baseline') and the skill level you wish them to achieve.

There are many different ways in which you can make step sizes even smaller. One of the most common techniques is to introduce prompts and different forms of help into the teaching, perhaps through the use of a classroom assistant or learning support assistant or by using a smaller group. The range of different sorts of help you can provide for the child is quite wide.

Verbal – giving verbal directions or reminders, perhaps giving the child the first sound when trying to think of the right word.
Demonstration – showing the child what to do as well as telling. This is particularly useful when the child has poor verbal comprehension, has behaviour difficulties or poor attention and is unable to respond to verbal directions alone.
Visual – any visual clues given to the child to evoke the correct behaviour, for example, pointing to the correct object for the child to choose; providing a yellow template for the child to trace over when forming letters or providing a number line for counting and simple calculation. Even at Key Stage 2, you can invent signs and symbols for correct behaviour or for remembering key points (full stops and capitals) and use it to point to rather than 'nag'. Inviting the child to use visual skills to correct mistakes is also an effective

approach, for example: 'See if you can spot the six spelling mistakes and mark them yourself with this red pen'.

Physical – anything done physically which evokes the response: for example, guiding the child through the part of the action too difficult for them to perform, such as rotating a screwdriver or forming the hand shape of a new communication sign. This may often prove a useful first step as the child needs to do little on his or her own and is therefore bound to experience success.

There are a number of other ways of reducing the size of your teaching steps. With tasks involving improvement in fine motor co-ordination, where perhaps the child can do a task but possibly not

very well, it may be useful to look at the *materials being used* and attempt to grade them. If you are teaching pencil control, you can start with chubby or triangular pencils and work on to finer ones that are harder to control. In tasks, such as sorting and matching, it can be helpful to present materials in such a way as to *reduce the difficulty of the choices* the child has to make and, therefore, the possibility that errors will be made. For example, if a child is learning to grade fractions in order of size, you can start with a simple choice of two and invite the child to indicate 'the bigger fraction' or 'the smaller fraction', moving on to providing more and more similar choices. Another way of achieving smaller steps is by looking at *the amount you require* the child to do. If you are teaching concentration, you can start with encouraging two minutes' independent work on a simple task and work up to ten minutes' independent writing, step by small step. On most occasions when you are doing a task analysis it is unlikely that you will be keeping to any single technique of making step sizes smaller. You can *mix and match* from the whole range of methods in order to ensure successful learning.

Differentiating targets

You have already considered how to write clear targets for IEPs on page 33. You can use the process of task analysis to break those targets down into simpler steps, which you can then teach to the child, week by week. The targets that you list when using a task analysis should be just as clear to everyone who reads them as those on the IEP itself. In reality, of course, you will have far more teaching targets for the child than those that appear on the IEP and the process of task analysis can be used for any teaching targets that seem to need additional or different approaches. Some targets are cloudy and give you no clear idea of what the child is doing now and what they *will* be doing when the target is achieved. For example:

● 'Jude will be less aggressive.' How will you know when you have achieved this?

● 'Molly's reading skills will improve.' What does this mean? Improve from what to what?

SPECIAL NEEDS **in the primary years:** Special needs handbook

Instead, aim for targets that are clear and measurable:
● 'Jude will work alongside the other children for ten minutes without attempting to poke them or use unkind language.'
● 'Molly will be able to read the first 100 high frequency words on our reading scheme without help.'

A clear teaching target will say what the child will do as a result of teaching under what conditions (for example 'with help', 'independently' or 'when asked'). It will not be written in terms of what the teacher will do ('Mrs Brown will hear Molly read every day').

Here is an example of how one teacher broke down the steps towards the IEP target for a seven-year-old girl with Asperger's syndrome (an autistic spectrum difficulty). There is a blank photocopiable form that you can use or adapt for breaking steps down on page 71.

Step-by-step planning

Name of child: *Yasmin*

Nature of difficulty: *Yasmin finds it hard to see the other person's point of view and to work co-operatively with other children.*

IEP target: *To work for ten minutes on a group task with three other children.*

Steps along the way:
1 *To play a simple dice game with LSA.*
2 *To teach game to Molly with LSA's support.*
3 *To play same game with Molly, Feras and Peter, LSA support.*
4 *To learn the 'Dinosaur concept game' with Feras and LSA.*
5 *To play it independently with Feras for three minutes.*
6 *To play it in same group of four, minimal LSA support.*
7 *To play a new game in same group of four, minimal LSA support.*
8 *To play a selection of games with a selection of pupils, 10 minutes, minimal support.*

Resources and support needed: *LSA during Daily Mathematics Lesson. Our usual range of Number Games including 'Snakes and ladders' and our 'Dinosaur game'.*

Help from parents or carers: *Yasmin and Mum to select a different game each week to play at home.*

Curricular area: *Ma2*

Date achieved: *16 May*

Developing a flow

The idea of differentiation has been around long enough now for most teachers to embed the principle into their daily practice. Differentiation is clearly about planning and organising teaching

tasks, resources and support. It also involves planning individual methods of assessment and feeding this back to the pupil so that learning is personalised. The idea is that the pupil gradually takes on more control of their own learning so that they begin to negotiate their own targets, plan what to do, take 'risks' in their learning and work with others on open-ended as well as prescribed tasks. To work effectively, IEPs need to feed into the short-term lesson planning in a flexible and fluent way. For skill-based areas of learning, you will find the task analysis approach particularly helpful. For other types of learning (such as more open-ended learning), you will find the broader approach in the curriculum framework the most useful. You may find the photocopiable sheet 'Lesson planning/differentiation'

on page 72 a good aid to your planning. Only some aspects of learning can be broken down into discrete, linear steps and your own expertise in teaching will help you to select, mix and match approaches for differentiation that will suit your situation and the pupils you work with.

Step by small step

Here is a checklist that you can use or adapt to help you make a learning activity more accessible for a child who has SEN.

● Can you make the whole learning activity easier for the child?

● Can you offer more help – for example, hand-over-hand to get them going, giving a point or a reminder?

● Can you reduce the distractions – for example, sit in a quieter area or offer less choice?

● Can you learn in a smaller group with an adult to support?

● Can you change the materials – for example, using a number line instead of counters?

● Could you expect slightly less of the child – for example, having a shorter story session?

● Can you plan more adult support – for example, a 'shadow' during outdoor playtime or a helper during PE?

● Could you build up the time gradually – for example, starting with only two minutes of concentration?

● Can you teach a new skill step by small step – try breaking down a written piece of work by first mind-mapping the ideas, then starting with the beginning, planning the end, and then finally adding the middle?

● Can you make an activity more rewarding or exciting – for example, by making sure it has personal relevance or interest to the child or adding an incentive such as a sticker?

● Can you rearrange the equipment or spaces, for example, so children can work at floor level or sit at a distraction-free work station for writing?

Step-by-step planning

Name of child:	
Nature of difficulty:	
IEP target:	

Steps along the way:	Curricular area:	Date achieved:
1		
2		
3		
4		
5		
6		
7		
8		

Resources and support needed:

Help from parents or carers:

Lesson planning/differentiation

Term:	Date:

Topic:

Core curriculum objectives:

Methods and approaches:

Resources:

Assessment opportunity:

Modification to include SEN:

Extension:

Checklist:

Are all learning styles catered for?

Is this realistic for the time available?

Is it relevant and personalised for this group of children?

Prerequisite skills needed:

MAKING SURE THE CHILDREN FEEL INVOLVED

The SEN Code of Practice emphasises the importance of involving children in your assessment and planning. This chapter explains how best to do this for all children.

Guiding principles

What should our overriding principles be when we work with children to assess and support their individual needs?

- Respect each child for their culture, their ethnicity, their language, their religion, their age and their gender. The methods we choose for assessment and intervention must be appropriate for the child. There must be no danger of bias.
- The care and education of children are not two separate, discrete activities. Therefore, when we work with children, we need to attend to their whole development and lives and not to certain aspects of it.
- Educational professionals inevitably have 'power' when working with children and their families; this needs to be acknowledged and used lovingly, wisely and well.
- Always keep the interests of the child paramount. Assessment and intervention must enhance their lives, their learning and their development. It must 'work' for the child.

Children's rights and choices

All children have a right to have their views taken into account in decisions about their education and progress. If you can find ways to involve them in decision-making it enriches their learning and helps them to develop life-skills such as problem-solving and negotiation. In the previous chapter, you considered ways that you could make learning more personalised for the child. In this chapter, we think about ways in which you can involve children with SEN in decisions about their learning, including ways of removing the barriers to learning they may face. Even if children have severe and complex needs, they will have views or feelings about the education and choices before them. You need to find innovative and creative ways to enable them to communicate their wishes to you, using specialist techniques if necessary. Over the next few years, you will receive more Government guidance on the approaches you can use as the 'Removing Barriers to Achievement' strategy is implemented.

Involving children in their own SEN monitoring

How can we involve children in their own assessments and interventions? For older children, we usually have the opportunity to talk and to listen, though it might take active planning to make sure that there is time and space to do this. For younger or differently abled children, we might not be able to talk directly about their needs and the kind of help they would welcome and our approaches may need to be less direct.

Involving children in reviews and target setting

You identified some ways of involving children in their own SEN approaches when you considered ways of gathering information prior to reviews (see page 39). In the same way, you can help children to set and break down their own targets and to express views about the kind of help they will need. There is a child-centred IEP on page 43. You might also find photocopiable page 77 helpful.

Talk-through approaches

Most schools have built up collections of stimulus books for covering a range of new situations the child might meet: going to hospital, having a new baby in the family or living with one parent. If you feel that you need a stimulus to introduce the subject of a child's SEN, you can develop your own resources along the lines of 'My Statutory Assessment' or 'Ali's Special Needs'. *Starting Out* (see page 96) is an approach for preparing a child with special needs for joining a new school. *Taking Part* (see page 96) provides a practical format for a parent or carer (or indeed a teacher or LSA) to lead a child through the process of statutory assessment.

Observation and interpretation

Take steps to stand back and observe the child in clear, objective terms: the level and range of their learning behaviour, the situations which encourage most interest or co-operation, and signs of pleasure and distress. We looked at ideas for observing children on page 21. Sometimes this enables you to work out what is motivating the child, what patterns there are to the learning and behaviour and what choices they make when left to their own devices. It can also help you write 'pen pictures', which are a powerful and child-centred way of portraying the 'essence' of the child to others.

Using play and free choice

We can observe the way children play with 'models' of their world and interpret how they are thinking about it, for example an older brother or sister playing with dolls, may act out considerable feelings of love, anger or fantasy after the arrival of a baby. Children can usually keep this behaviour separate from real life and use it to deal with strong emotions without developing the behaviour at home. Older children use drawing and art in a similarly cathartic way.

Ways of aiding communication

If a child lacks language or the skill to convey appropriately how they are feeling, look for alternative methods. Offer a choice of 'objects of reference' (coat/cup/paintbrush/number line) and ask the child to indicate which activity they would like to do next. Use photographs or symbols to represent the school day to show a child what comes next or invite them to choose the order in which they complete tasks. You might find photocopiable page 78 helpful to copy and adapt for talking to children. Decide on your questions (for example, 'This is how I feel when…' or, 'This is what I think about PE'). Start with simple, non-threatening questions and then move

into more sensitive areas if you need to. For some children with very poor communication skills, you might wish to put together a 'communication book' showing photographs of the child in different moods and explaining to new staff or supply teachers, 'This is how Georgie looks when she is feeling ___'.

Children's drawings

Children's drawings have been used extensively in assessing developmental levels, emotional states, achievement and personal experiences. They can act as a springboard for further talking and thinking together. In a similar way, we can use our own drawings and illustrations as a stimulus for children's own comments and interpretations, for example, 'What is happening in this picture? Is it right or wrong?' or, 'Can you draw a line on this piece of paper to represent your life like this – let's put in the important things that have happened since you were born'. This, too, will give us a glimpse of the way children understand their worlds.

Personal profiles

Personal profiles can be adapted and developed in order to gather information about the child's view and progress as they move through school. These might include child-centred questionnaires about successes, achievements and challenges over the year, leading into target setting for the next class. They might involve pieces of work selected by the child to 'keep forever' or photographs and reports. You might find the *All About Me* materials (see page 96) very helpful here and these can also be used as part of gathering information for a child with SEN.

Photographs and ICT

Another way in which adults can obtain a child's-eye view of school life is to provide a digital camera and encourage a child to take photographs of things that are important to them. Piece together a picture of children's priorities and impressions by collating evidence from the children and adding the views of parents and colleagues. You can also help children develop IT skills in producing their own class booklet for newcomers or for parents and carers.

Child-centred approaches

As part of making your assessments and interventions meaningful and child-centred, look for ways of 'starting where the child is at' and 'going with the child', aiming at all times for the child to feel comfortable and encouraged by the assessment process itself. Develop the spirit of 'let's find out about how you do this', rather than 'what you can or cannot do'. We should aim to make our assessment involving, pleasurable and positive for the child. Assessment should arise naturally from a routine and familiar situation in which the child is enabled to show off their abilities as well as their level of need. This is most likely to happen in spontaneous learning arising from the opportunities that you have set up in your class.

Talking to *all* children about SEN

Make sure that the teaching materials and books within your class reflect a wide range of ability, ethnicity, and culture. Books that contain 'models' of differently-abled children and adults can act as talking points and establish disability as part of everyday life. Most libraries have now developed specialist sections of books that relate to a wide range of special needs. As well as covering certain conditions, there are books that will appeal and be helpful to younger or differently abled children at certain stages of exploring and talking, such as 'multi-sensory' or 'interactive' books. You will find some SEN book specialists listed in the resources section.

Making everyone feel included

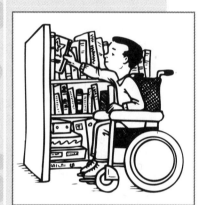

In order to ensure that *all* children can learn, you may need to modify the physical structure of your classroom. Think about the arrangement of furniture and fittings to ensure physical access, storing resources at child-height for the child who cannot walk, the use of soft furnishings, carpets and curtains to absorb sounds, or floor-level learning where appropriate in order to include a child with sensory or physical difficulties. Colour-coded areas and organised storage systems help with putting away and finding again and encourage independence. Symbols can be used to help children with communication difficulties to express choices or understand what comes next in a sequence of activities. 'Sandwiching' short structured activities with free play can make it easier for the child with attention difficulties to concentrate for longer, together with opportunities to think and play in quieter, distraction-free areas. Specialist tools can be obtained for making computer equipment accessible to all children (see page 95). The opportunity to work in large and small groups, and sometimes individually, can again provide opportunities for *all* children to learn in a variety of situations and through a range of different learning styles.

Building confidence

From the youngest class, you can encourage children to develop confidence and help them feel settled and secure around other children. We know that children develop confidence fastest if they have caring and supportive adults to encourage and guide them and when they are helped to take risks, learn from their mistakes and work independently to achieve success.

Confidence and learning seem to be bound together; if children try something and succeed, self-esteem and confidence are raised, and they are likely to try again next time. If they try something and feel a sense of failure, self-esteem and confidence are lowered and they are less likely to try again. That is why our approaches to SEN have to be positive and encouraging. We must make sure that the activities we are providing are at just the right level for success, even if a child has significant learning difficulties. Using circle time on a regular basis is a useful way to make sure that each child feels included and valued and allows you all to share pleasure and fun at the same time.

Daily targets

My name is: _____ **My class is:** _____

Today's date is: _____

My targets for today are:

1

2

3

This is the help I need to reach them:

Signed:

Was I successful? Here is my sticker:

How do you feel?

WORKING WITH PARENTS AND CARERS

Parents, carers and professionals should work in partnership in order to meet children's SEN. This chapter suggests practical ways of establishing effective home–school links.

Education and support

We all believe that the interests of children are paramount in schools. It is now also recognised that children need stability and security if they are to succeed in school and as citizens of the future, and that parents and carers should be aided in supporting their children. Over the next few years, you are likely to see more national parent helplines, an enhanced role for health visitors, additional support for parents to learn with their children through family literacy and mentoring schemes, introduction of education for parenthood as part of the school curriculum and more support for grandparents. There are also moves to provide better financial support for families through initiatives, such as benefits and tax allowances, with national strategies to help families balance work and home, and links with a move towards more family-friendly employment rights. These proposals have led to the development of various community and parenting education programmes throughout the country. There was a tendency in the past to develop 'top down' parent training courses in which professionals determine what they feel parents and carers should know. One example of this is the provision in the Crime and Disorder Act (Home Office 1998) to order 'parenting classes' for parents/carers of offending youngsters. Thankfully, there is now also a trend towards more 'bottom up' parent education, which is broader, has more of an open access and

is based on what parents and carers want to know. 'Parenting education' has tended to develop in the voluntary sector in response to consumer demand. Before designing any parent education or training, find out what already exists in your area and ask what works for whom and how. Increasingly, parents and carers are being given the right climate to enable them to develop a real voice in what they need for their children. Look on this as a good opportunity for working in partnership and sharing your expertise as an educator with their needs for the best in their family's education.

Parental responsibility

It might be helpful at this stage to define the terms 'parent' and 'parental responsibility'.

All those with parental responsibility for a child have rights and responsibilities towards the child. If a child is subject to a care order, this is shared with the local

WORKING WITH PARENTS AND CARERS

authority. A school should involve all those with parental responsibility as much as possible in the child's education. However, if this is not possible or practical, the school may discharge its responsibilities by dealing with the parent who has day-to-day care of the child, such as the foster parents of a child 'looked after' by the local authority. The school should ensure that all parents and carers have information regarding the SEN policy and arrangement for their child's SEN.

Definition of 'parent'

Section 114 (1D) of the Education Act 1944, as amended by the Children Act 1989:
Unless the context otherwise requires, and in addition to the general definition, a 'parent' in relation to a child or young person includes any person:
● who is not a natural parent of a child but who has parental responsibility for them, or
● who has care of the child.
Definition of 'parental responsibility'
Section 2 of the Children Act 1989:
Parental responsibility falls upon:
● all mothers and fathers who were married to each other at or after the time of the child's conception (including those who have since separated or divorced)
● mothers who were not married to the father at the time of the child's conception, and
● fathers who were not married to the mother at the time of the child's conception, but who have obtained parental responsibility either by agreement under the Children Act or through a court order.

Parent partnership

The involvement of parents/carers at all stages is a basic principle of the SEN Code of Practice. In Chapter 4, you read about the various services that LEAs must now set up to keep parents and carers informed and supported whilst SEN procedures are being followed for their children. There are also requirements for schools to forge closer working links with parents and carers. Schools are required to draw up 'home–school agreements' which explain the school's aims and values, its duties towards the pupils, the responsibilities of parents/carers and what the school expects of its pupils.

What approaches seem to be effective for developing a real partnership between parents and education professionals?
● You need to acknowledge the fundamental role that parents and carers have already played and continue to play in their child's development and education.
● Look for ways of sharing the responsibility for learning between home and school. This is done through mutual respect, ongoing communication and regular information.
● Make sure that parents or carers feel welcome in your classroom at the end of the school day and that there are opportunities for working together with parents, staff and children.
● Parents or carers need information at all stages of their children's learning and progress (and not just when there is a 'problem').
● Admission procedures should be flexible to allow time for discussion with parents/carers and for children to feel secure in a

WORKING WITH PARENTS AND CARERS

new class. Here are some ideas for helping you communicate effectively with parents/carers when talking about their child's SEN.

Handling feelings with sensitivity

When a child first starts in a new class, it is a difficult time for all parents and carers. Add to this the particular concerns and mixed emotions which parents of a child with SEN might have, and you can understand that sensitive handling will be vital for effective partnership with parents. When parents or carers are first told that their child might be disabled or have special needs, they can experience a whole range of overwhelming emotions. There are often feelings of inadequacy, bereavement, anger and grief. To this can be added denial and helplessness. It helps if you can try to 'tune in' to some of these emotional reactions that you might be picking up from a parent. There may be feelings of guilt ('what did we do wrong?'). There may be a tendency to blame or they may not trust you to cope. Parents/carers may be hanging on your every word in case they feel that you are rejecting their child. Try to understand all this if, at first, a parent/carer seems defensive or 'prickly' towards you. Even though the family might have lived with the concept of 'SEN' for some years, mixed and confused feelings can still surface whenever there are new issues concerning their child's progress.

Talking with parents/carers

What can you do to become as sensitive as possible to parents'/carers' feelings and emotions?

- Try to understand why parents/carers might be saying something. What does this tell you about the way they are feeling? One way to do this is to think about how they are making you feel at that point in time. If they make you feel angry, they are probably angry themselves and you need to defuse the situation by not adding to the confrontation until things are calmer. If they make you feel sad, they may be depressed and need your nurturing and understanding. If you are left confused, then they are probably feeling very muddled themselves and need your clear information and guidance. If they are making you feel anxious, then that is probably just what they feel too.

- Share clear information about your curriculum in order to inform parents/carers about what you hope to achieve for their child at each age and stage. It is helpful if parents and carers are involved in the learning wherever possible so they can see what you are trying to achieve, particularly for those children who have SEN.

- Helpless or troubled parents need practical workable advice, but not the impression that the professionals are the successful ones and they, the parents, are failing. Parents with low self-esteem and high stress are quick to pick up the fact that they are 'not doing it right'. This leads to resentfulness and avoidance.

- Instead, home–school activities should be negotiated, and suggestions need to be encouraging and warm, for example: 'What seems to keep his attention at home?', 'What would be good for building her concentration?' and, 'What help do you need from us?'

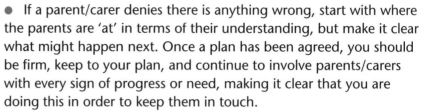

● If a parent/carer denies there is anything wrong, start with where the parents are 'at' in terms of their understanding, but make it clear what might happen next. Once a plan has been agreed, you should be firm, keep to your plan, and continue to involve parents/carers with every sign of progress or need, making it clear that you are doing this in order to keep them in touch.

● If a parent/carer cannot or will not stop to talk, try to negotiate a home visit to meet on their home territory. Start by finding out what their views and feelings are; this gives important information to you about how you can introduce your own concerns.

● Do not be tempted to see parents as 'over anxious'. Parents'/carers' views should always be taken seriously, and reassurance should be given, with evidence that all is well.

● Sometimes parents/carers might realise there is a problem, but refuse any kind of outside help, even though the teachers are convinced that things have come to that stage. Explain how it is *you* that need the outside advice and support in order to provide the best help for their child – this avoids the suggestion that there is something 'wrong' with their child. If necessary, agree to do your best without outside help at one review meeting, but agree in advance that you will refer the child to an outside professional at the next review meeting if the targets have not been met.

Choosing the right words

Invest time before a child joins your class gathering information and establishing a relationship with the child and parents/carers. A home visit can be very helpful, sharing photographs of your working day and talking about your typical activities. Asking positive, open-ended questions can provide information about the child's strengths and about the kind of help that they need. Parents/carers soon feel discouraged if they find themselves listing all the things their child cannot do. Take time to ask parents/carers what they would like the school to do to help, making sure they are not left feeling that they have failed in some way. Taking trouble to share the 'good news' from the start helps any 'bad news' to fall more into context.

Developing a practical partnership

Here are some practical ways of involving parents or carers in meeting their child's needs.

● Invite parents/carers to school. For various reasons, parents/carers do not always call in to school on a regular basis, even when it is a parents' evening. It is often helpful to invite parents/carers personally into school to share information about their child's achievements, in an informal way, or even to arrange a home visit if necessary.

● Draw parents'/carers' attention to a display where their child's work can be seen. Make sure that there is something to celebrate.

● Before you dwell on difficulties, show parents what their child has already achieved and improvements to their behaviour made within your class. Do not make them feel too despondent if there have not been the same improvements at home. Use the 'good news' as a hope for positive changes to come.

WORKING WITH PARENTS AND CARERS

● Ask the child to show their parents/carers what they can do or what has been learned. Make sure that any homework has an element of showing off a new skill or success to parents or carers as well as being something more challenging.

● Ask parents or carers for their opinions by providing opportunities for them to contribute information and to share their experiences with you. It is often helpful to set aside a regular time when other demands will not intrude.

● Thank parents or carers regularly for their support.

● Celebrate success with parents/carers. This will ensure an ongoing positive partnership.

● Use a home–school diary to keep in touch. A two-way system of sharing information about a child's success, experiences and opportunities can help in supporting the child. Make sure that you are aware of any literacy or translation needs for the families you are communicating with.

Sharing home plans

One useful way of developing a practical partnership with parents or carers of a child with SEN is to negotiate a home plan to share with parents. This contains ideas for supporting their child's learning at home. The home plan can link in with the child's individual education plan (see page 43).

Home plan

Home plan for: Luke

Date: Monday 4 May

IEP target: For Luke to form his letters correctly.

Aim: For Luke to form the letters a e i o u correctly.

Getting started:

Help Luke to hold his pencil correctly, using the triangular pencil grip. Sit beside him and guide his hand as he makes rows of the letters. Talk him through it as he writes the letter: 'round, up and down' (and so on). Give lots of praise and show how pleased you are.

Now make the letter shapes in a yellow felt-tipped pen (again with the pencil grip) and give him a darker pen to form the letters on top of yours. Show him where to start each time.

Activities to try:

* When he is getting better at it, ask him to cover a sheet of paper with different coloured letters to make a pattern. Bring it in!

* Have fun playing a game where he traces one of the letters on your back and you guess what it is.

* Breathe on mirrors and make the letter shapes.

* Trace them in water or a soap solution on the kitchen-counter top — anything to get him to practise the shapes!

* Write L_k_ and encourage him to fill in the u and the e. Think of other familiar names where he can do this for the other letters too.

How to help

As Luke becomes more able, reduce the amount of help you give until he is managing to form the letters correctly all by himself.

The example on the previous page and below is a home plan for Luke, a seven-year-old boy with general learning difficulties. The first sheet is completed by the teacher and is shared with parents and carers who take it home and try out the ideas. The second sheet is completed by parents and carers who comment on how well Luke has managed the learning task on each day. They then bring the sheet back to share with the teacher and discuss what the next steps might be.

Home feedback

How did _____ Luke _____ get on?

Monday	We got a new set of felt-tipped pens for him, but all he wanted to do tonight was draw with them, so we let him.
Tuesday	He let me hold his hand and do letters for about five minutes then got fed up.
Wednesday	Today Luke managed the e all by himself, with only a little help to get started! I said he could go and watch TV as soon as he's done his work and this seemed to help.
Thursday	He loved the guessing game on my back and got really good at it.
Friday	We were out at Beavers.

Is there anything you would like to talk to the teacher about?

I noticed that Luke has a lot of difficulty remembering where to start with the a. How can I help him?

You will find a blank home plan and home feedback sheet to photocopy or adapt on pages 85 and 86. You might like to photocopy the home plan and the home feedback sheet back-to-back to make it more convenient to use. You might also find the sticker charts on pages 87 and 88 helpful to link in with your home targets. A sticker supplier to fit this size of space is listed on page 96. Explain to parents/carers that once a sticker has been given it should never be removed, whatever the child does next. This is because a sticker is a real sign that the child did what was required at that moment in time and under the child's own volition and control. This helps children learn that they have the ability to learn and improve by themselves and feel pleased with their own achievement, rather than to do things that keep adults pleased.

Home plan

Home plan for:	
Date:	
IEP target:	
Aim:	
Getting started:	
Activities to try:	
How to help:	

Home feedback

How did _____ get on?

Monday	
Tuesday	
Wednesday	
Thursday	
Friday	

Is there anything you would like to talk to the teacher about?

My sticker chart

My target:

I was given a sticker each time I managed this!

My sticker chart

My target:

I was given a sticker each time I managed this!

WORKING WITH OTHER AGENCIES

This chapter discusses ways in which you can work co-operatively with other agencies and professionals who can give specialist advice and support you, the family and the child with SEN.

Joining up

The new Government strategy 'Removing Barriers to Achievement' (see page 94) describes how we can all work together to improve the partnership between different agencies and professionals. From time to time, you are likely to find that your school will be asked to take part in a self-evaluation of how inclusive your provision is and how you work jointly with others. There will be SEN regional partnerships which enable best practice to be shared between different authorities. You will also see the development of children's trusts that bring together services for children across social services, education and health.

This can only serve to help parents and carers of children with disability and SEN who at present find themselves working with a bewildering array of different professionals and agencies. Teachers are ideally placed to help parents and carers pull together all the information and advice they have, drawing it into an IEP that is both practical and, where necessary, based on multidisciplinary advice. In this chapter, you will read about some of the agencies and outside professionals who might be able to support you, the family and the child and who might have an input into the IEP.

Support services

The school's SENCO will have collected information and contact details for all the professionals and services that might be able to support you. Here are some starting points. Find out from your SENCO who your contact might be, what sort of help they can offer you, at what level of concern you can contact them, and how you can access their services.

Support teachers

Learning support teachers have developed a special knowledge of children's learning difficulties, how to assess these and interventions that usually prove to be effective. Most will usually advise in general ways when children are being monitored at School Action, though a referral system usually operates for direct involvement at School Action Plus. They have particular knowledge of the statutory assessment procedures and are therefore well placed to talk you through the process. They are often on hand to visit schools and help staff develop individual teaching programmes for any children with SEN. Sensory support teachers have specialist qualifications in teaching children with very particular needs, such as hearing impairment, visual impairment, or multi-sensory difficulties. Other

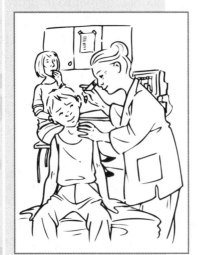

support teachers may specialise in autistic spectrum difficulties, communication or speech and language difficulties. Behaviour support teachers have a special knowledge of how children behave and how you can plan ways of encouraging more appropriate behaviour or overcoming emotional and social difficulties. Some teachers are involved in directly teaching children individually or in small groups, in cluster centres or at home. Contact your LEA or talk to your SENCO for details of the referral systems for your area.

Community doctors and paediatricians

The paediatrician works with parents and carers to identify the cause and diagnosis of a medical condition. Paediatricians and community doctors also have a role in providing or arranging genetic counselling when necessary, and in tapping into in-patient facilities. Paediatricians also provide the service of monitoring medical conditions and needs as the child grows older, and checking hearing and vision is an important part of this. Community doctors (who often double as school doctors) can help to liaise with teachers where you need information about how to manage a child's condition in school, and can assist with the statutory assessment of SEN. Referral is usually via the school nurse, health visitor, child health clinic or GP.

Speech and language therapists

Speech and language therapists offer assessment, treatment, advice and counselling to people of all ages with a speech, language or communication disorder and related eating and swallowing problems. They also offer support and advice to educational professionals to help them understand the nature of a child's speech, language or communication problem and how they can help. Referral is usually via the GP or sometimes the SENCO.

Physiotherapists

Physiotherapists can elect to specialise in children's work. Their aim is to work towards helping the child reach their maximum potential. An individually planned programme of physiotherapy might cover careful positioning and movement, advice and support, special handling skills, exercise regimes, walking practice, balance and co-ordination exercises, stretching of muscles, chest physiotherapy and special equipment. They work particularly with children with physical disabilities and delay, providing information on handling and care, lifting, positioning, nasal suctioning, inhibiting abnormal reflexes and advising on splints, boots, braces, wheelchairs and buggies, sometimes overlapping with the occupational therapist. They also work with certain medical conditions, such as cystic fibrosis, providing exercises and daily therapy programmes. Referral is usually via the paediatrician, GP or sometimes the SENCO.

Occupational therapists

Occupational therapists work with children of varying ages whose development or independence is interrupted by physical,

psychological or social impairment or disability. They aim to develop the child's maximum level of independence, thereby improving practical life skills, which hopefully promote a better quality of life. They assess gross and fine motor skills, any dyspraxic difficulties, writing skills, independence skills, visual perception and body awareness, and the need for specialised equipment for home and pre-school, including seating, wheelchairs, toilet and bathing aids and adaptive equipment to improve everyday skills. Sometimes they can advise on the handedness of children who cannot sort it out themselves. Referral is usually via the GP or sometimes the SENCO.

Clinical psychologists

Clinical psychologists offer family support and counselling, family therapy, advice and intervention on attachment difficulties, cognitive and developmental assessment, advice on behaviour management, and specialist knowledge of certain conditions, such as autism. They work within health service settings, usually in child and adolescent mental health services or learning disability services. Referrals usually come through GPs or sometimes a social worker.

Educational psychologists

Educational psychologists are employed by LEAs and assist in finding solutions to learning difficulties, problems or needs. They usually work within an educational psychology service (EPS) and often service a cluster of schools in one area. Sometimes they accept individual child referrals from SENCOs and provide individual assessment and advice. Increasingly, they now work on a consultative level, discussing children's needs in school, perhaps doing assessment as well, but aiming to work together with others to make a difference to children's happiness and progress. They help by clarifying and defining the problem, generating teaching and management approaches and evaluating the success of these. They can provide specialist assessment of all kinds of learning difficulties, and advice on behaviour management is often given. An educational psychologist will always become involved if a child is being statutorily assessed.

Social workers

Counselling and family support are given, usually with home visits, to assess or support the family situation. They have access to social services provision, including family workers, respite care, shared caring, and other support schemes. Child protection procedures are also a crucial and specific role, as is dealing with the possible conflict that this can raise for some families. Referrals usually come through the duty officer at the local social services office.

Confidentiality

Working with outside professionals can sometimes raise tricky issues of confidentiality. Here are some pointers.
● The information from professionals in the health services will be confidential so don't be surprised if it cannot be sent directly to you.

WORKING WITH OTHER AGENCIES

● The best practice is to access any medical information or reports that you need to know through parents and carers if they agree. Otherwise, if this proves problematic, contact the local school nurse or community doctor for advice.

● Never copy other professionals' reports without permission.

● Keep all confidential reports in a locked cabinet and operate a 'need to know' policy for sharing sensitive information (such as information on HIV/AIDS).

● Never promise absolute confidentiality to a child, parent or carer. You need to make it absolutely clear that your involvement can be confidential unless you see the need to protect the child or report criminal activity.

Dear Colleague
Joint-planning meeting

Name of child:
Date of birth:
Address:
School:
Class:

As you may know, this child is due to join this school/class on:

We are holding an initial planning meeting to help us plan the best approaches.

Day:
Time:
Venue:

The purposes of this meeting will be:
* to gather and share all relevant information
* to hand over between professionals
* to help us to plan our approaches
* to learn about what approaches have helped in the past
* to learn who can be called upon to help in the future
* to set up good communication for the future
* to reassure and support staff who will be in direct contact with the child
* to address potential difficulties early on
* to detail the need for any specific resources from outside the setting.

We do hope you can attend, or perhaps send us any information that might be helpful. We are looking forward to welcoming this child and to providing the best support we can.

Yours sincerely

Joint planning

When a child with disability or SEN transfers into your school or class it can be invaluable to hold a planning meeting in order to help people think through the needs of individual children and how these might be met in your class. Do not wait to be invited to one; set this up yourself if you feel it would be helpful. The SENCO should be able to give you advice or co-ordinate this for you. You will find it best to contact professionals well ahead, asking:

● if they feel it would be useful to come

● if they would contribute a report

● suitable times.

You can then find a date that suits most of you, making sure that it also suits parents or carers.

This letter suggests what purposes such a planning meeting could serve.

Now that you have reached the end of this book, you should be feeling familiar with most of the basic terms used when talking about special educational needs. You should find the 'Jargon buster' on page 93 helpful as a reminder for yourself, as basic training to support colleagues, or as a handout for parents and carers.

Jargon buster

Autistic spectrum disorder – a collection of difficulties related to poor communication skills and isolated behaviour.

DfES (Department for Education and Skills) – provides guidance for schools on how to put Education Law into practice.

Differentiation – breaking activities down or coming at them in a different way to ensure successful learning.

Disability – having a long-term physical or mental impairment that affects day-to-day activity.

Dyslexia – a specific learning difficulty affecting reading and/or writing.

Dyspraxia – a developmental difficulty in co-ordination.

Equal opportunities – making sure that all children can have the same opportunities regardless of gender, ethnicity, ability or faith.

Foundation Stage – education from three to five years old.

IEP – individual education plan.

Inclusion – including everyone together.

KS1 (Key Stage 1) – education for five- to seven-year-olds.

KS2 (Key Stage 2) – education for seven- to eleven-year-olds.

LEA (local education authority) – your local education office.

LSA (learning support assistant) – a non-teaching assistant.

P Scales – targets for children still learning at an early stage.

Parental responsibility – any parent who still has legal responsibility for a child.

QCA (Qualifications and Curriculum Authority) – provides guidance to schools on the curriculum to be taught and how to assess.

School Action – action taken by a school to meet a child's SEN.

School Action Plus – action taken by a school planned with outside professional advice on the child's SEN.

Self-esteem – how happy you feel with yourself.

SEN (special educational needs) – any needs that require additional or different approaches to usual.

SENCO (special educational needs co-ordinator) – the school's teacher who advises colleagues on SEN and co-ordinates how SEN are met.

SEN Code of Practice – the document that tells LEAs, schools, governors and SENCOs how they must meet SEN.

SENDA (the SEN Disability Act) – states how schools must plan to include children with disabilities.

Statement – an official document stating what a child's needs are and how the LEA will meet them. It is only used for the most severe or complex cases of SEN.

Statutory assessment – the process of gathering reports in order for an LEA to decide if a statement is going to be necessary.

RECOMMENDED RESOURCES

GOVERNMENT GUIDANCE

● *The National Curriculum: handbook for primary teachers in England Key Stages 1 and 2* (DfEE and QCA, www.nc.uk.net).

● *The National Numeracy Strategy* (DfEE, ref NNFT, www.standards.dfes.gov.uk).

● *Supporting the Target Setting Process* (DfEE ref 0065/2001, www.standards.dfes.gov.uk) – all about P Scales.

● *SEN Code of Practice* (DfES ref 581/2001, www.dfes.gov.uk).

● *SEN Toolkit* (DfES ref 0558/2001, www.teachernet.gov.uk).

● *Inclusive Schooling: children with special educational needs* (DfES ref 0774/2001, www.dfes.gov.uk).

● *The National Literacy Strategy* (DfES ref 0500/2001) and *Early Literacy Support Programme* (DfES ref 0650/2001, www.standards.dfes.gov.uk).

● *Accessible Schools: planning to increase access to schools for disabled pupils* (DfES ref LEA/0168/2002, www.dfes.gov.uk/sen).

● *The National Literacy and Numeracy Strategies: including all children in the Literacy Hour and Daily Mathematics Lesson* (DfES ref 0465/2002, www.dfes.gov.uk).

● *Code of Practice for Schools* (Disability Rights Commission, 2002, www.drc.gov.uk).

● *Planning, teaching and assessing the curriculum for pupils with learning difficulties* (QCA, 2001, www.qca.org.uk)

● *Removing Barriers to Achievement* (DfES ref 0117/2004, www.teachernet.gov.uk/wholeshool/sen/senstrategy)

NATIONAL ORGANISATIONS

● **ADHD Family Support Group,** 1A High Street, Dilton Marsh, Westbury, Wiltshire BA14 4DL.
– For advice and information on attention deficit/hyperactivity.

● **Alliance for Inclusive Education**, Unit 2, 70 South Lambeth Road, London SE8 1RL. Tel: 020 7735 5277.
 www.allfie.org.uk.
– Campaigns to end compulsory segregation of children with special education needs within the education system.

● **Barnardo's,** Tanners Lane, Barkingside, Ilford, Essex IG6 1QG. Tel: 020 8550 8822. Fax: 020 8551 6870.
Website: www.barnardos.org.uk.
– Provides care and support for children in need and their families, with projects throughout the UK.) Also send for their publication list: Barnardo's Child Care Publications, Barnardo's Trading Estate, Paycocke Road, Basildon, Essex SS14 3DR.

● **The Child Psychotherapy Trust,** Star House, 104–108 Grafton Road, London NW5 4BD,
www. childpsychotherapytrust.org.uk.
– Produces several 'Understanding Childhood' leaflets covering emotional and mental health issues: send for a catalogue.

● **Children in Scotland,** Princes House, 5 Shandwick Place, Edinburgh EH2 4RG, tel 0131 228 8484,
www.childreninscotland.org.uk.
– For training and information.

● **Children's Society,** Edward Rudolf House, Margery Street, London WC1X 0JL, tel 0845 300 11 28, Website:
www.the-childrens-society.org.uk.
– Works with children in need and their families, for example in independent living projects for children leaving care and home-finding projects for children with special needs. Runs several family centres and parenting projects.

● **Contact a Family,** 170 Tottenham Court Road, London W1P 0HA, www.cafamily.org.uk.
– Produces on subscription the 'CaF Directory of specific conditions and rare syndromes in children with their family support networks'. Provides support for parents.

● **The Department for Education and Skills** (DfES), Website: www.dfes.gov.uk.
For parent information and for Government circulars and advice including the SEN Code of Practice.

● **The Down's Syndrome Association**
www.downs-syndrome.org.uk.
● **The Parent Network**, 44–46 Caversham Road, London NW5 2DS, 020 7485 8535
● **Makaton Vocabulary Development Project**, 31 Firwood Drive, Camberley, Surrey GU15 3QD, tel 0127 661 390, www.makaton.org.
– Information about Makaton sign vocabulary and training.
● **MENCAP**, www.mencap.org.uk.
– Support organisation for children with severe learning difficulties and their families.
● **National Association for Special Educational Needs**, NASEN House, 4–5 Amber Business Village, Amber Close, Amington,
Tamworth, Staffordshire B77 4RP.
Tel: 01827 311 500, www.nasen.org.uk.
– Professional association with a database of relevant courses for those wishing to train in SEN; also runs training courses itself.
● **The National Autistic Society**, Willesden Lane, London NW2 5RB. Helpline telephone: 020 7903 3555. Website: www.nas.org.uk.
● **National Children's Bureau**, 8 Wakley Street, London EC1V 7QE, 020 7843 6000, 020 7843 6008 (library enquiry line: 10am–12 noon, and 2–4pm).Website: www.ncb.org.uk.
– A multidisciplinary organisation concerned with the promotion and identification of the interests of all children and young people. Involved in research, policy and practice development, and consultancy.
● **National Council of Voluntary Child Care Organisations**, Unit 4, Pride Court, 80–82 White Lion Street, London N1 9PF. Website: www.ncvcco.org.
– Umbrella group for voluntary organisations dealing with children. Ensuring the well-being and safeguarding of children and families and maximising the voluntary sector's contribution to the provision of services.
● **National Society for the Prevention of Cruelty to Children** (NSPCC), National Training Centre, 3 Gilmour Close, Beaumont Leys, Leicester LE4 1EZ, www.nspcc.org.uk
– For training on SEN, child protection and family work.

● **Royal National Institute for the Blind** (RNIB), 105 Judd Street, London, WC1H 9NE, 0845 766 99 99, www.rnib.org
– Send s.a.e. for resource list and toy catalogue.
● **Royal National Institute for Deaf People**, 19–23 Featherstone Street, London EC1Y 8SL. Tel: 0808 808 01 23, www.rnid.org.

EQUIPMENT AND RESOURCES
● **Acorn Educational Ltd**, 32 Queen Eleanor Road, Geddington, Kettering, Northants NN14 1AY, 01536 400 212, www.acorneducational.co.uk
Equipment and resources including special needs.
● **Fisher-Marriott Software**, 58 Victoria Road, Woodbridge IP2 1EL.
Tel: 01394 387 050.
Website: www.fishermarriott.com
– For 'Starspell' software.
● **CSIE** (Centre for Studies on Inclusive Education)New Redland, Frenchay Campus, Coldharbour Lane, Bristol BS16 1QU, http://inclusion.uwe.ac.uk.
– Publishes *Index for Inclusion: Developing Learning and Participation in Schools* by Booth, Ainscow, Black-Hawkins, Vaughan and Shaw.
● **Don Johnston Special Needs**, 18–19 Clarendon Court, Calver Road, Winwick Quay, Warrington WA2 8QP. 01925 256500, www.donjohnston.co.uk.
– Produces the 'Solutions for Pupils with Special Needs' resource catalogue, full of intervention resources.
● **KCS**, FREEPOST, Southampton SO17 1YA, www/keytools.com.
– Supplies specialist tools for making computer equipment accessible to all children.
● **LDA Primary and Special Needs**, Duke Street, Wisbech, Cambridgeshire PE13 2AE. Tel: 01945 463441, www.ldalearning.com.
– Supplies *Circle Time Kit* by Jenny Mosley (puppets, rainstick, magician's cloak and many props for making circle time motivating).
● **Lucky Duck Publishing Ltd**,
0117 973 2881. www.luckyduck.co.uk.
– Send for a catalogue of videos, SEN books and resources, especially for behavioural and emotional difficulties.

● **The Magination Press**, The Eurospan Group, 3 Henrietta Street, Covent Garden, London WC2E 8LU, www.maginationpress.com.
– Specialises in books that help young children deal with personal or psychological concerns. Send for a catalogue.

● **NES Arnold**, Novara House, Excelsior Road, Ashby Park, Ashby-de-la-Zouch, Leicestershire LE65 1NG, 0845 120 45 25 www.nesarnold.co.uk
– Supplies the *All About Me* materials by Sheila Wolfendale, which can be used to involve children and parents in the assessment process.

● **nferNelson**, Tel: 0845 602 19 37. Website: www.nfer-nelson.co.uk.
– Send for their Specialist Assessment Catalogue.

● **The Psychological Corporation**, 01865 888 188, www.harcourt-uk.com.
– Produces a catalogue of Educational Assessment & Intervention resources.

● **Super Stickers**, P.O. Box 55, 4 Balloo Ave, Bangor, Co. Down BT19 7PJ, www.superstickers.com.
– Produce stickers for reward and motivation.

● **Quality for Effective Development** (QEd), The Rom Building, Eastern Avenue, Lichfield, Staffs WS13 6RN, www.qed.com.
– Publishes the books *Taking Part* and *Starting Out* by Hannah Mortimer.

● **SBS (Step by Step)**, Lee Fold, Hyde, Cheshire, SK14 4LL, tel 0845 300 10 89. www.sbs-educational.co.uk.
– Supplies toys and equipment for all special needs.

● **White Space Ltd**, 41 Mall Road, London W6 9DG. Tel: 020 8748 5927, www.wordshark.co.uk.
– Supplies the 'Wordshark' software.

● **Winslow**, 0845 921 17 77, www.winslow-cat.com.
– Send for their Education and Special Needs Catalogue.

BOOKS FOR ADULTS

● *Effective Teaching and Learning in the Classroom – a Practical Guide to Brain Compatible Learning* by Sara Shaw and Trevor Hawes (Optimal Learning series). Available from Optimal Learning, P.O. Box 12, Leicester, LE2 5AE, 0116 279 1111, www.optimal-learning.net.
For helpful information on learning styles.

● *Turn Your School Round* and *More Quality Circle Time* by Jenny Mosley (LDA). Available from LDA, Duke Street, Wisbech, Cambridgeshire PE13 2AE, 01945 463 441, www.ldalearning.com.

● *Disability Equality in the Classroom: a Human Rights Issue* by Richard Rieser and Micheline Mason is published by Disability Equality in Education (which also provides training and booklists suitable for children): Unit GL Leroy House, 436 Essex Road, London N1 3QP. Their resources catalogue is available from the website, www.diseed.org.uk.